What Others Are Saying about This Book...

"*The Aspiring Actor's Handbook* tells it like it is... what it takes to live the life of an actor. More than just talent—it takes guts. Be prepared. Know what's ahead in this life you've chosen. Knowledge is power. Read the book. Enjoy the journey. Good luck."
—**Bryan Cranston, actor, 3-time Emmy Winner, star of *Breaking Bad*; *Argo*; and, *Malcolm in the Middle***

"*The Aspiring Actor's Handbook* is full of wisdom, humor and honesty. More importantly, it shows that there is a place of success for actors between the 'starving' actor and the 'star.'"
—**Donald Petrie, Director, *Miss Congeniality*; *How To Lose a Guy In Ten Days*; *Grumpy Old Men*; and, *Mystic Pizza***

"This book can absolutely create more harmony and love for the 'show business' you want to be a part of. I wish I had had this advice when I was starting out." —**Dee Wallace, actress, star of *E.T.*; *10*; *The Howling*; and, *The Hills Have Eyes***

"It's good to know there is a resource to show fledgling actors that there are many paths to a successful and fulfilling career."
—**Howard Murray, Director, *The Big Bang Theory*; *Grace Under Fire*; and, *Harry and the Hendersons***

"Zipp and Cheek are wonderful actresses who write about the logical, but not always obvious, aspects of acting as a business, and it being not just a career, but a lifestyle. It felt like I was having a conversation with old friends. Two thumbs up!" —**Mariko Ballentine, theatrical agent (Minc Talent), and 30-year veteran of casting and teaching**

"Reading *The Aspiring Actor's Handbook* is like spending a wonderful afternoon with a group of caring professionals who bring you into their inner circle of show business and give you a glimpse of the good, the bad, and the many s~~urprising possibil~~

D1566502

ities in between. Like big sisters, Debbie Zipp and Molly Cheek encourage young actors to ask the tough questions, face the stark realities, and still hold onto their dreams with integrity and individuality." —**Elizabeth Browning, actress, acting coach and Producer of *The Face***

"A must read not only for any actor starting a professional career but also for the veteran actor. This collection of voices from the community of working actors offers frank advice and inspirational anecdotes. Acting can be a lonely profession, but with this book in hand you'll never feel alone." —**Jan Bina, Actress, *Troop Beverly Hills*; acting teacher; and, casting associate**

THE ASPIRING ACTOR'S HANDBOOK

What Seasoned Actors Wish They Had Known

With Workbook and Discussion Guide

Molly Cheek and Debbie Zipp

BETTIE YOUNGS BOOKS

Cover Design by Adrian Pitariu
Text Design by Jazmin Gomez

Bettie Youngs Books are distributed worldwide. If you are unable to order this book from your local bookseller or online from Barnes & Noble or Amazon, or from Espresso or, from Read How You Want, you may order directly from the publisher.

BETTIE YOUNGS BOOK PUBLISHERS
www.BettieYoungsBooks.com
info@BettieYoungsBooks.com

Print ISBN: 978-1-940784-12-0
ePub ISBN: 978-1-940784-02-1

Library of Congress Control Number available upon request.

1. Cheek, Molly. 2. Zipp, Debbie. 3. Bettie Youngs Books. 4. Acting. 5. Acting Careers. 6. Media. 7. Publicity. 8. Self-esteem. 9. Movies. 10. Film. 11. Broadway. 12. Training to be an Actor. 13. Television. 14. Actors and Actresses. 15. The Motion Picture Industry. 16. The Television Industry.

Printed in the USA

Table of Contents

Acknowledgements

We would like to thank the many stellar professional actresses who shared their experience, wisdom and stories for inclusion in this book. Your contributions are an invaluable asset. We respect you as extraordinarily talented, savvy women and friends. We know first-hand the sacrifices you have made for your art and admire your strength, courage and perseverance. Though some may not live the lifestyle of the rich and famous, you are passionate about your work and continue to honor and better yourselves as artists! And for that, you are true professionals.

To our husbands, our families and our friends: thank you for all the ways you supported our work on this book. You are much appreciated and loved.

A big debt of gratitude goes to Mariko Ballentine, Cheryl Benton, Jan Bina, Robert Lane, Emma Lee, Susan Lehman, Pat Lentz and Lee Murphy for taking the time to read our book in the early stages and bless us with your encouraging comments and insightful advice: What a difference you made!

We also wish to thank our publisher Bettie Youngs of Bettie Youngs Book Publishing and her staff for their belief in us and for their role in helping us bring this book to light. Thank you for all your work in helping us to launch our book!

CHAPTER 1

So, You Have Been Bitten by the Acting Bug!

Good for you—and welcome aboard! Whether you have come bursting onto the acting life straight out of high school with stars in your eyes, or trained extensively at college, acting school, or, have just tinkered with community theatre, whatever the case, we applaud you for the courage to pursue your dream. But, starry eyes and a few credits won't be all you'll need. We know from experience that you will also need some guidance and advice!

An actor is an artist, and the life and career of an actor is very different from a 9-to-5 job. It may not be as easy to accomplish as you may think. Perhaps it is not as hard as you think. Pulling off a successful career that pays your bills and offers enjoyment and fulfillment is not an easy endeavor. But, it is possible. And we're here to help.

Acting isn't just your job, it is an art.

You've probably already heard plenty of advice from well-meaning people such as your mother, your high school English teacher, or a good friend. Thanks to the abundance of celebrity media these days, many people think they are qualified to give advice on a wide range of show business topics, when probably, they are not. So what is a budding actor to do, and who do you need to listen to as you begin seeking work in the field of acting?

As seasoned actors, we have something realistic and constructive to share with you about becoming an actor. While we, the authors and contributors to this book, refer to ourselves as actresses, the insights we share are universally applicable to aspiring performers, male and female. We have been in your shoes, and our collective and combined experience exceeds our thirty years of individual experience.

There are scores of books, websites, and blogs on the craft of acting, auditioning techniques, how to get ahead and the like, but there is so much more to know about creating and sustaining a full life as a working actor.

You Can Have a Successful Acting Career— Without Being a Star

As professionals who have experienced a great deal of success, we are here to tell you (and your doubting family, friends and loved ones!), that there exists a vast middle ground between being a "starving artist" and having the success of an Angelina Jolie. Yes, it IS possible to have a rewarding and balanced life as a working actor. You can make a very nice living and have a normal life, even if no one outside of the business knows your name—and that is success.

When we look back over our careers, what we missed most was a mentor, someone to tell our younger and inexperienced selves just what we are going to tell you. From experience, we can tell you that coaches, agents and teachers just aren't enough to fully arm you to face the mighty challenges in front of you. As those who have "been there," we can offer you real-world perspective that will help you as you move forward.

The two of us came to our acting careers from different parts of the country and with different backgrounds. Our stories and experience from our life as actors is a bit different—but what we have most in common is our love of acting and our ability to have been able to make a living in our careers. The tips, advice and personal stories we are about to share are heart-felt and given with respect as you begin your journey pursuing your dream. In that spirit, we share what we know—and what we wish we had known when we were starting out.

We want you to feel comfortable trusting us as we express our opinions and stories with you throughout these pages. So, we'll each share an overview of our careers, the basis of our experience and where we're "coming from." You will also be hearing from twenty-five very special, well-seasoned actresses who have a lot to add to your understanding of the working actor's life.

Alright, let's begin!

An Overview of Our Acting Experience

MOLLY CHEEK: I was raised in the suburbs of New York and spent the first 10 years of my life bugging my parents to take me to see a Broadway musical. I got my wish with the original production of *Oliver*, followed by *The Sound of Music*. Not a bad era to start a love affair with theater. In school, I tried out for every production my various schools mounted, from *H.M.S. Pinafore* (Tokeneke Elementary) to *Six Characters in Search of an Author* (The Thomas School for Girls). And, I spent summers and weekends in various theatrical programs. Even so, it never occurred to me to consider acting as a profession. That was just fun, not something people other than Bette Davis did for a living. It seemed so out of my reach.

At Connecticut College, I tried out for every play—and majored in Government. Two days before graduation, Fred Grimsey, the man with all the keys on his belt who ran tech on all the shows, asked me what I planned to do after school. I shrugged and said something about maybe applying to law school.

"But you love to act, right?" he asked.

"Yes," I responded.

"You're 22. Why not try doing what you love for a few years and if at age 25 it's not working out, then go to law school?"

"Hmmmm," I thought. So, I got a job in dinner theatre in Nashville that summer, which led to a few tours through the South, and then proceeded to summer stock in Terre Haute, Indiana. I eventually wound up in New York—where I took my first acting class. I made the rounds of agents and booked a lot of commercials while catching up on technique and skills.

Once I felt I'd mastered commercial "acting," I felt confident to move into television. I landed a few small parts in movies made for TV, which inspired me to set out for Los Angeles for a pilot season. If only because of the bravery it took to leave everyone and everything I knew behind, the trip was victorious.

Once in Los Angeles, I tested for a few pilots, but didn't make the cut. I went back to New York and immediately got called back to Los Angles for the mini-series, *Breaking Up is Hard to Do*.

In fairly quick succession, I was cast in a short-lived series, *The Yeagers*, where I was thrilled to work with a childhood idol, Andy Griffith. As you can imagine, this was heady stuff. "Wow," I thought, "I'm not *watching* Andy Griffith on TV—I'm ON TV with him!" Next came 13 episodes of *Chicago Story* where I co-starred with Craig T. Nelson and Dennis Franz.

Still, gratifying as every job was, I had my heart set on sitcoms since falling in love with *The Dick Van Dyke Show*. So when I landed a co-starring role on the uber-hip *It's Garry Shandling's Show,* everything seemed to come together. It was the first time I really set my sights on a specific role, even uncharacteristically bringing a bag of props to the final callback—which paid off in spades.

Those four years were the most stimulating and affirming in my working life. What a privilege to work with writers at the top of their games and incredibly creative actors—not to mention all the celebrities who made cameo appearances.

Another wonderful gift of long-term employment followed with three seasons of *Harry and The Hendersons*, life-long friends, and, a fabulous husband (whom I connected with again years later) were the great rewards there.

After seven consecutive years of full-time work, suddenly, my employability was revoked. At forty-two I was too old for television.

It was a terrible blow to me because I had flourished for so long in show business only to come face-to-face with a retirement for which I was unprepared emotionally and financially. I had never had any other job. There were no other skills to fall back on. Worse, who was hiring forty-two year-old "trainees?" And besides, what other work would I even want to do? All these were tough questions at the age of forty-two.

Little did I know then, that ultimately, they'd be as empowering as my initial move to Los Angeles. I enrolled in a chef training course, and began a small catering and gift basket business. I reinvested in my acting career by going back to class and doing plays—which, by the way, was an experience I'd missed on the way to a TV career. I took in roommates. I re-evaluated a lot, and I joined a support group of women experiencing the same devastating lack of work, Actresses@Work. Having never been a joiner or particularly fond of other actresses, it was a big step, but again, life-changing.

But, often one positive step leads to unexpected possibilities. I got a last-minute call from my agent to fill in for an actress who had reneged on a role in a low-budget film called *East Great Falls High*. Grateful for the few days' work—even though it wasn't a script I could write to Mom about—it was work. Imagine my surprise to open the *LA Times* Calendar section months later to see my picture splashed across the front page, extolling the hilarity of the newly-titled feature film "American Pie."

Miracles do happen.

DEBBIE ZIPP: I hail from Overland Park, Kansas, so my only exposure to "Show Business" was our TV. The deep desire and motivation and the blind passion I had started when I was only five years of age. I will always remember something of that moment. We lived in Independence, Kansas, and my Dad was a Sunday school teacher. One day I accompanied him to the show being presented by our church. I remember sitting next to him and how I was overcome by an intense and uncontrollable desire to be on that stage (or altar) and I really caused a scene.

Being a very well-behaved child up to this point, this was totally out of character for me. I kept trying to thrust myself out of my seat, up the aisle to the altar (to me a stage)—my Dad doing his best to restrain me. Since I was only five, I don't remember getting in much trouble, but boy-oh-boy do I remember that intense, innocent and unexplainable desire. I certainly didn't know what I was going to do up there, I just wanted desperately to be up there and play with the people on stage.

Right after that, I was enrolled in several dance classes to appease my urges. In junior high, at age thirteen, I was cast in my first play as the 70-year-old character "Ma" in the short play, *It's Cold in Them Thar Hills*. Well, that sealed the deal; my path was clear to me and my parents.

I have to say that I learned the most about acting in high school from my wonderful high school drama teacher, Robert Lane, and from my speech teacher, Sally Shipley, as well as my Finishing School teachers at "Patricia Stevens." I learned a lot from many teachers that followed, but the words of support and encouragement and the tools of acting I got while in high school stuck with me and became the solid foundation of my craft. I took every opportunity to be on stage that I could, from drill team, dance recitals, speech contests, musicals like *Hello Dolly* in which I played Ermengarde to Antigone in Anouilh's version of *Antigone*. Also of much help was the acting in numerous scenes with the stars of the popular TV shows of the time like, *The Man from U.N.C.L.E.* and *I, Spy*—all played in front of the mirror in my bedroom!

In 1970, after graduating high school, I came to California to attend a Performing Arts College to get a Bachelor of Fine Arts in Acting in San Diego. There are many things I wish I had known and could have told that young determined but inexperienced girl of eighteen—who had never been away from home! Many years later my Dad told me that as he was driving away from the college after situating me in my dorm, he desperately wanted to turn around and fly me back home with him to Kansas. But he stopped himself, thankfully! I will be eternally grateful to him for that. If he had come back, I would have gone home with him because I was so terrified. But, if I had gone back home, my life would have been filled with regret.

From that point on it was full steam ahead because my desire to be an actress was so strong.

The Performing Arts College in San Diego did prove to be a stepping-stone and a great training ground. I received my Bachelor of Fine Arts from U.S.I.U. School of Performing Arts. One of the teachers at USIU set me up with an agent, and I moved to Los Angeles. It wasn't long before I was cast in a lead role in the television series, *The Cheerleaders* (not the infamous porno film!).

This was right about the time I got married, and soon thereafter, my agent called with the news that I had landed my first National TV commercial. This opened a whole new world for me. Doing TV commercials provided me with a good living and health insurance—and at that point, allowed me to be selective about the acting parts I took in my theatrical film and TV acting career.

I never had to do odd jobs again.

Throughout my acting career, I did over 300 national television commercials. I had leading stage roles in Los Angeles which included Judy in the Victory Theatre production of *Sirens of Seduction,* Gracie in *Let's Call the Whole Thing Gershwin* at the Westwood Playhouse (now known as The Geffen) and Debbie in *The Good One* at the Pan Andreas Theater.

Beside lead roles on stage, I had a lead series regular role in the TV Pilot *There's Always Room* playing opposite the renowned Maureen Stapleton. I also starred with Darren McGavin in the series *Small and Frye* for Disney. I guest-starred on many TV series including *Magnum PI*; *Paper Chase*; *LA Law*; *New Love American Style*; *One Day At a Time*; *Gilmore Girls*; and, *Malcolm in the Middle*. I appeared in numerous films including "*Like Father Like Son*; *One Day And A PC*; and *Double Exposure*. As a side note, of all these, I'm probably best known for my recurring lead role as Donna in the *Murder She Wrote* series starring Angela Lansbury.

So I made a darn good living at my chosen profession—until I made the ultimate Hollywood faux pas: I turned 40!

Sad but true, the opportunities for work as an actress from forty years of age or older, diminish greatly for the majority of working actresses. Of course there are exceptions, especially if a woman is an established star, but nevertheless, ageism is prominent in the entertainment industry. I started seeing the auditions dwindle—and soon I wasn't making a decent living. It was a shock and, to be perfectly honest, it broke my heart.

On the bright side, it is amazing how my acting skills translated into other skills that I found rewarding. In those years when my opportunities for acting jobs were rare I discovered all kinds of new abilities, passions and dreams I wanted to pursue. To further the cause of improving the images of women over forty in the media, I joined the support group for actresses that Molly did (Actresses@Work) and after a few years, became president of that group. For the next three years, I discovered and used my leadership skills as well as my activist skills—merging them with my creative skills as an actress. To pursue my new love of producing, I co-founded the for-profit production company IN THE TRENCHES PRODUCTIONS. My partners and I felt the best way to bring change to an ageist industry was to create media content that would reflect the lives of women over forty.

As an actress, I had to learn to overcome and adapt to all kinds of situations, and perform professionally at the top of my game. This prepared me for how I needed to conduct my life. The experiences of my acting career have prepared me for a lot of the challenges I've had to face in my life.

Sadly, in 2007, I chose to retire from acting. My teenage son became very sick with a rare illness, and he needed my full attention. By this time I had already mourned my dwindling career because the opportunities and the juicy roles had been fading away, so it was easier to walk away. But that said, even if my career had been on a huge roll at the time my son got sick, I still would have retired to take care of him. I was also very blessed that my husband was making a living that supported our family.

I also found that my acting skills and my ability to quickly access my emotions and passion came in handy when dealing and coping with the doctors, medical technicians and the health insurance company. It was the role of a lifetime: "Mommy Warrior."

It took three full years for my son to be well again, but I still have not gone back to acting. At this point, I'm not sure if I'll ever go back. The desire to create a role of substance overwhelms me now and then, but less often. It is a journey of self-discovery now.

I've done some great roles and had a lot of joys in my work and a certain amount of success. I've worked with some great actors and actresses and made life-long friends. I have a wonderful life with my husband, two grown children and all my friends.

Still, nothing can take away from the fact that I made a living for three decades doing what I loved!

I count myself lucky.

CHAPTER 2

To Be or Not to Be an Actor—That is the Question!

If you haven't already, you are going to hear from family and friends how they feel you should, (or shouldn't), go about becoming an actor. "You have to go to Juilliard;" "Never do soap operas or commercials;" "You can't make a living at that;" "A manager is essential;" or, "It's all about who you know,"—all well-intentioned advice. While some may actually know the business, most won't, even though they think they do because they've watched shows like "Entertainment Tonight."

Despite all the good intentions and often helpful information, the bottom line is there is only one way to have the career success you want, and that is, YOUR WAY!

That is not to say that you shouldn't stay open to advice that resonates with you. Just recognize and honor your own instincts first and foremost. When all is said and done, no two actors will follow the same path. No two actors will be presented with the same opportunities in just the same way, nor at the same time or stage of his or her career. No two actors will use the advice given by their various teachers, agents or mentors in the same fashion. But, in every single circumstance you encounter, your best guide is your own gut. It's honoring your individuality and trusting your instincts and remaining true to yourself that matters most.

As you circle the decision to pursue an acting career, we strongly advise that you first think about what a commitment to this profession means. You need to approach it with eyes wide open.

The primary caveat is this: many people want to be actors, but there just isn't enough work to go around. Forget stardom; just earning a living is extremely rare. In fact, it's common knowledge that only 1 to 2 percent of those lucky enough to be eligible for SAG/AFTRA membership—or who are already members—make a livable wage acting. The statistics show that some 98 percent of union actors have to hold another job in order to finance their desire to perform.

Making peace with that truth is essential to a realistic grown-up perspective about your quest for an acting career. You must also be really honest with yourself about your ability to flourish in a free-lance lifestyle. You will most likely need a job to support your pursuit of being an actor. You have to be willing to do that. In our opinion, making a real living as an actor means you are able to pay all your bills and meet your financial responsibilities from your earnings as an actor and ideally, have savings to see you through a year of not working.

Even if you make a living acting you are rarely employed consistently. Acclimating to the sporadic nature of this work is not something everyone can do. Plans are frequently jettisoned for a last-minute audition. Financial obligations must be carefully parsed so the sudden loss of financing for that film you've been cast in or that stage play you were going to start rehearsing doesn't throw you into debt. Your ego can feel like a yo-yo on a daily basis, losing one job and getting a callback for another within minutes. Be truthful about answering this important question: Will you be able to maintain a healthy balance in the chaos and insecurity of a show business career?

Clearly, a profound passion for the work and a solid belief in yourself and your talent are the most essential tools to drive you forward and face what are bound to be plentiful obstacles to your success. Only you can know how much you want this career, and what you are willing to sacrifice to have it.

Success Traits Necessary to Show Business

DEBBIE: There was definitely a moment in high school that should have discouraged me but didn't even register in my mind. I had to do a career report in my senior year, and I got a meeting with Hal Holbrook when he was in Kansas City performing "Mark Twain." How I got that interview with him I will never know. Hal Holbrook was lovely, but he was very discouraging about the odds of making it as an actor. He truly gave it to me straight. For any teenager with the slightest doubt in their heart and mind about their chosen risky path it would have made them turn to another career goal. But, it didn't faze me. I believed I was the one who would make it. My desire and focus were not to be deterred. If anything, I was more emboldened. So my decision and path from that point on was very clear to me.

MOLLY: Having never known anyone who actually tried to be an actor, I came in kind of assuming it was an impossible goal. As far as I was concerned, it was a shot in the dark I was willing to take, and then follow it as far as it led. I believed the odds were preposterously stacked against me, but I consciously decided not to think about all the competition or how unlikely success was because if I did, I wouldn't even begin the journey. So, I put on the blinders and plunged ahead. A fortunate side note was that I never had to battle my parents over my decision to pursue acting. Whether out of indifference or because my Dad worked with actors doing commercials—or because I never asked for their financial help along the way—my parents didn't seem horrified by the dim prospects. So, I felt free to go where I needed to.

DEBBIE: My daughter—who now has her own thriving artistic career in another medium—when she was much younger, complained that I had never encouraged her to be an actress.

MOLLY: I didn't know she wanted to be an actor.

DEBBIE: Neither did I! She said that in high school she had a desire to be an actor. She thought she would be good at it but never got any sign of support for entering the acting field from my end. "Hmmmm…" I said, "maybe I didn't encourage you because you never told me you wanted to be an actor."

MOLLY: Hellllooooo!

DEBBIE: "Maybe because you never joined a drama club or asked to take an acting class or never tried out for a school play?" However, I told her, "Even if you had told me and even if I wasn't supportive, nothing I did or didn't do should have mattered to you. Nothing would have stood in the way of your passion for acting and pursuing it. Once I discovered that love, nothing would have stopped me." So I told my daughter, "Then you didn't want it bad enough."

MOLLY: It was never do or die for me. It was the job I most wanted to do. Something that always stuck with me was my college roommate's grad school application essay, where she said the reason she wanted to pursue social work was that it was the thing she felt best about herself doing. And that's how I felt and what helped me justify choosing such a "self-centered" profession. I never thought I was Meryl Streep, or that if I couldn't perform I'd wither and die. I just liked myself most when I was acting. So I decided to see how far I could pursue it. Not a very romantic approach, but certainly a practical one and probably helpful when it came to not taking the rejections personally.

DEBBIE: I think your attitude at that time is the more healthy approach. If you hadn't succeeded as much as you did, you might have just moved on to another profession with fewer tears than I would have. However, you were one of the lucky ones who were successful relatively quickly. But, I think for most of us, at least for me, the desire needs to be strong. It has to be powerful enough to compel you to leave the safer career choices behind for this unknown and mercurial profession and to sustain you through the journey. No matter what I went through in this pursuit, it was always only a brief, passing, barely noticeable thought to leave the acting profession for something more secure. And whether it is your approach or mine or another way, finding the connection with acting that feeds you, fortifies and validates your commitment to stick with it till you see what is possible for you as a professional actor, is the important thing.

MOLLY AND DEBBIE: We've asked some of our colleagues and friends to weigh in on this. Here is some important insight and words of advice from some of the motion picture industry's most successful actors.

Insight and Sage Advice from Well-Seasoned Actors

"My first Business of Acting Coach, Wayne Devork, said, 'If there is anything you would rather do or are interested in, then do it.' This is a career that chose me. I have tried many times to find a different career, a different passion, but I keep coming back and didn't give it up. Maybe I was naïve about it, but I thought I had a choice in the matter. As it turns out, I was genetically programmed to be a performer as far back as I can remember." —**ROBERTA BASSIN**

"There is an anecdote that when a young George Clooney asked the legendary director Joshua Logan what his advice was to an actor starting out in the business, his reply was, 'If something can talk you out of this, let it.'" —**JAN BINA**

"If you'll do it for free, you do it because you love it. That's how I feel about acting." —**ROBIN POLK**

"If you have the passion and drive for this career, then set your goals now. Let them inform your career decisions. At age 24, I set my career goals: longevity, variety and consistent work. They still hold true for me today." —**MARIANNE MUELLERLEILE**

"When I was twenty I living in New York City and studying to be an actress. While I was working as a dancer, my desire and my focus was so strong and bright, there was no way that it couldn't happen for me. I savored the life that I had chosen (it was fun!) even the heart-breaking drama of not getting a role, since that led to even more desire on my part to succeed. All this in hindsight since I remember one major rejection put me in bed for three days!" —**MURPHY CROSS**

"You have to want to be an actress with every fiber of your being. If you have any doubts or think you need something to fall back on just in case the acting thing doesn't work out, do something else. There are too many dedicated and talented actors out there who want nothing else and will do anything to achieve their dream. I never wanted anything else, and I knew I would be successful if I put all of myself into my acting career. I rallied my parents behind my dream, and they became my biggest fans." —**ANNE MARIE HOWARD**

"Back when I was living in Houston, Texas, I had a wonderful acting coach, Chris Wilson. On my first night in her class she asked if anyone in the room would really like to become a working actor. It took everything in me to raise my hand because I never had anybody support my dream. But I did it. I raised my hand. It was so liberating. I finally gave myself permission to say yes to my dream. She looked out at us and saw that some of us had the balls to raise our hands, and she said, 'You can, you know. You can become an actor.' It was the greatest gift anyone had ever given me. I would love to pass this permission along to your readers. Yes, you can become an actor. But you have to pursue it because your soul will give you no rest unless

you do, because it's not easy, but if you love it, it won't be work."
—**MAGGIE EGAN-CUMMINGS**

"Stay focused. Do NOT give up your dreams, but be wise in choosing what is really meant for you. Not everyone is going to be a successful actress, but everyone has the opportunity to be a successful person." —**IONA MORRIS**

"A guy writing an article for the arts section of the newspaper once approached me. He asked me if I would talk about the drinking and partying. I remember laughing out loud and then feeling quite offended. What he had no understanding of was how disciplined a stage actor must be. I tried to explain that, in order to perform eight shows a week, there is no way that you can be drinking and doing drugs. When that curtain goes up, it's on you; no second takes! And as for partying, when other people go out, you have a show, when others go out of town for vacation, you have a show. When others get together for the holidays, YOU have a show. Understand that. Make friends with that. You have to love the theatre more than you love anything else. Or don't go into this business. A reputation of being disciplined, dependable, and devoted is the most important calling card you will have."
—**BARBARA DIRICKSON**

CHAPTER 3

Breaking In

As daunting as it feels not knowing how you will ever get your career started, the fact that you never know where your break will come is also a gift, because it can come from anywhere. There is no universal, magic key to the kingdom. Everyone finds a different way in. Some actors start with a college degree, some begin right out of high school. Some start in theatre, others do commercials, or TV, or films first. Some go to New York, some to LA, and some wind their way through regional theaters. There is no right place to start and no formula for finding your first break. It's wide open, so all you can do is be available and prepared so that when that break finds you, you will be ready.

We share our own abbreviated experiences as a way to reinforce the fact that you don't need to know anybody or have gone to the right school to embark on the acting career you've dreamt of having. Every single working actor found their own individual route in and realized their dream a different way. What they all have in common is that they kept at it. They kept trying everything, every way.

So, just put one foot in front of the other, and keep your eye on the prize.

Getting Your Foot in the Door

MOLLY: It was scary for me to figure out how I would ever get my foot in the door. Unlike my husband who grew up in a show business family, I never knew anyone who could show me the ropes. When I moved to New York, I had exactly one "contact"—a casting lady at an advertising agency where my father once worked.

DEBBIE: Oh, that was good.

MOLLY: Unfortunately, her specialty was in the modeling world and Cindy Crawford I'm not. Nevertheless, as a courtesy to my Dad, she set me up with a meeting at Wilhelmina. While I was sitting in the waiting room feeling horribly out of place, two of their male clients dropped in to chat with their agents and proceeded to double-team the obvious newbie—me. They started teasing me and quizzing me about my "credits." I guess I kept up with them well enough to pass some kind of muster because one of them wound up taking me under his wing and introducing me to the agents who ultimately shepherded me through the first five years of my career. He did this knowing he hadn't a clue if I could act my way out of a parking ticket. He was just in a good mood—and thought I was cute. And voila, I had an agent!

DEBBIE: Wow! A stroke of luck that he was in a good mood, BUT you were the one that passed the test.

Being from Kansas, not thinking I had enough training and, of course, no clue how to start an acting career, I opted to go the college route. I remember the circumstances of my audition for that performing arts school in San Diego, and I don't know how I did it. I had to perform two monologues, dramatic and comedic in a tiny cramped hotel room at a Holiday Inn in Kansas City with both the representative from the Performing Arts College and my father in the room. They were so close to me while I was performing my super-dramatic monologue from the Greek play "Antigone" by Sophocles, that my spit was probably hitting them directly in the face the entire time. I can honestly say the uncomfortable circumstances of that audition didn't faze me.

I would be horrified to try and make my monologues sing in a stuffy small hotel room with a stranger and my Dad right there. If I had to do that today or any time after my 30's, I may not have had the courage. As for that seventeen-year-old self, I didn't give it a second thought because I wanted it that badly. But, I got accepted. And while there, one of my teachers (who had more than a few connections) picked a handful of students from all his classes to meet an agent in Los Angeles. I was one of the chosen, and she took me on and was my agent for many years. So when I moved to Los Angeles, I was lucky because I already had an agent.

That was my path, and I would say that was my first break. After I graduated college that agent was responsible for getting me the audition that was to be my first job.

MOLLY: My first paid work was in dinner theatre in Nashville—a most unlikely scenario, given that I had never even heard of dinner theatre. Nor had I imagined living anywhere but New York City. My college acting teacher was home for the summer and had gotten the gig directing a dinner theatre show and offered me a role, and one long bus ride later, I was acting for money! Well, room and board and tips, but that was okay for me at twenty-two years old.

I was always embarrassed about the year I spent on tour with the shows packaged from there because I thought "real actors" would never do that kind of schlock. Thinking about it now, I realize how silly I was to imagine someone just starting out could be expected to have major theatrical credits right out of the box. Where else could I have worked except lower level venues? So, when I ultimately got to New York, I presented those credits as Summer Stock, which sounded classier to me.

DEBBIE: Really, and as far as anyone who looked at your resume was concerned, a credit is a credit is a credit. I don't think there is much difference between Dinner Theatre and Summer Stock. It is all a paid, out of town theatre gig. It is splitting hairs really. It is not like you made something up, which I would never recommend. You just tweaked the name.

MOLLY: Right. Who cared where you got the credits as long as you could come up with the goods at your current auditions. I just always worried I didn't have the same amount of training and experience my peers had gotten by majoring in Theatre or something. And, personally, the dinner theatre chapter of my life was really rich and eye-opening.

DEBBIE: I was very lucky with my first job. I had just finished my college credits with an apprenticeship at Missouri Repertory before I moved to Los Angeles to pursue my dream. I worked as a file clerk to pay the bills and wasn't getting many auditions and certainly no acting jobs. So, I moved to San Diego when a gig as a singing waitress came along, figuring I could just commute for auditions in Los Angeles, which is a perfect example of the sacrifices you must be willing to make to break into this business.

San Diego is good distance from Los Angeles, and it took a lot of juggling and road time to make it work. But, about a year out of college at an audition, I got the lead in a television pilot for NBC and 20th Century Fox called *The Cheerleaders* directed by Richard Crenna. I also became a member of SAG. So I didn't start out doing a small walk-on part and then working my way up the ladder, so to speak. I started my career with the funny lead character in a television pilot for a major network!

It was kind of shocking but I certainly wasn't complaining. It was a copy of *Happy Days,* which was a huge TV success at the time, only my show centered around high school girls. I was 21 playing a person who was fifteen. Everything about it was perfect. I loved being the funny comic lead sidekick! It was such a dream come true—a complete joy! I wanted to do that every single day of my life. I was so terribly disappointed when it didn't sell and make it to the fall lineup, and I had to go back to the singing waitress job. But that is show biz. However, it gave me a taste of the real thing and motivated me to move back to Los Angeles. Once there, using my savings. I started on a path to being a comic actress.

Insight and Sage Advice from Well-Seasoned Actors

"I created my first big break myself! I was teaching high school in Kansas City, Kansas, and came across an article in the New

York Times re: Hal Prince looking for an 'unknown' to star in *A Little Night Music*. I wrote him a very cheesy letter about a new kid from Kansas and took an even cheesier picture and sent them off with wild dreams of becoming a star.

Lo and behold, his assistant called me three weeks later, saying that Mr. Prince was taken with my letter and would like to fly me in! Being the honest young lady I was raised to be (albeit stupid in this moment), I announced that I already had my ticket, and Mr. Prince didn't have to spend the money. So my first day in New York City, after a harrowing plane ride in coach from Kansas City, I put everything I had into a cab, gave the driver the address to the apartment I had not even seen yet, and made my way to Rockefeller Center to audition for Hal Prince.

I made it to the last five girls after the dancing and acting. Then the announcement came: 'Mr. Prince would like to hear you sing now.' I gulped, I blinked, and then I stammered, 'I'm sorry. I didn't know we had to sing.' The silence filled the room. Pause. Then, very gently, his assistant said, 'Well dear, it IS a musical!'

And so my very first day in New York City, I sang Happy Birthday for Hal Prince. When the musical director asked the key, I replied meekly, 'Somewhere in the middle?' Needless to say, I did not book the part. But by the time I left that Rehearsal Hall, I had a list of the top voice teachers, acting coaches, and dance studios from all those wonderful girls who looked at this very green newcomer and decided to mentor and befriend her.

Six years later I was starring in *E.T., the Extraterrestrial*. I often wondered if Hal Prince kept track of that the girl from Kansas who didn't have a song when she tried out for the musical!"
—DEE WALLACE

"When I started my acting career, I had a degree from UCLA, a lifetime teaching credential—and, was married and had two preschool children. I had been a dance and exercise instructor, and an elementary and adult education teacher in the Los Angeles Unified School District. My fellow actors were all single and had been actors straight out of college or before. People follow their dreams at different stages of life. My first big break came

when I auditioned for the role of Lilly, opposite Mickey Rourke and Faye Dunaway. I was just beginning. I had no credits to speak of. In the waiting room I thought to myself, 'What do I say if they ask me what I have done?'—which they did! I answered in character as the irascible 'Lilly' and said, 'Who wants to know?' Director Barbet Schroeder and producer Fred Roos got all excited and asked me to read. In my innocence, not knowing one doesn't touch or invade their space, I grabbed a glass off the desk and told them what I wanted to read in the script and went for it! Barbet, in his Swiss French accent, said, 'She's Lilly, she's Lilly!' When the audition was over, and I went out of character, we all laughed. At home I received a personal call from the casting director, Nancy Lara, 'You're their number one choice and you beat out Cloris Leachman, Madeline Kahn and Sandra Bernhard for the role!' This casting director's office had found my headshot at the bottom of a box under a desk, and the rest is history."
—ROBERTA BASSIN

"Everyone has his or her really motivating story and this was mine. It was during college and I had my heart set on New York and being a Broadway singer and dancer. My first stepping out into the professional arena was an interview with a 'big' theatrical casting director. A friend of a friend set up a general meeting with this man (who must not be named), and in my fantasy (fantasies are good), who was going to discover me and my amazing talents and make me a star. No pressure! I sat down on the couch in this 'snake's' office in a run-down building in Hollywood and spent the entire 15 minute interview (felt like hours) holding back the tears and defending myself from the humiliation of a very abusive male who thought he had the power to destroy an overly enthusiastic young wanna-be actress and enjoyed every bloody moment of it. He proceeded to tell me that my look was 'average;' my speaking voice was 'street;' and that I hadn't studied at the 'right' conservatory. And, he said, that even if I could sing and dance, that wouldn't be enough to build a career on and he was certain I couldn't act due to my southern-splashed street speech. There was just no way I could become a serious professional actress, and I should forget about it. He then offered, out of the goodness of his heart, to pull some strings and get me an audition for the chorus of a small touring company headed for Mexico. I'm not kidding! I left that room and could not even stand up outside the door. I literally fell to the floor, my Scarlett O'Hara moment, and vowed 'As God is my witness, I WILL BE A SUCCESS!' In that moment I made the decision and mustered the courage to succeed in my craft! Find the courage inside you, put on your big girl panties, and you Go Girl!" —**SHERRY HURSEY**

"1964, and the morning after graduating from The University of Tulsa in Oklahoma I was on a Greyhound bus to New Hampshire to apprentice in summer stock with the Peterborough Players. Three months later I was back on the bus on my way to my new life in New York City. People have always told me I had great timing, but this trip turned out to be my best timing ever. A friend who had graduated the year before was on Broadway in the original *Hello Dolly* company. And lo and behold a month after I arrived, Gower Champion was putting together the international company starring Mary Martin. My friend thought I was perfect for the role of Ernestina Money and begged Gower's assistant to let me audition, even though I was non-union, had no experience and had never sang or danced before! Fortunately the hierarchy in this company enjoyed giving new kids a helping hand. So there I was, standing on a Broadway stage in front of Gower Champion! I read the scene and moved on to my song. And what did I do? Started on the wrong note! Fortunately I was too naive to care, and didn't really know who Gower Champion was, so I simply shifted up to the right key in mid-song. At the end I saw Gower coming down to the stage, and naïveté ruling again, simply said 'That what ya want?' He laughed and said, 'Yes.' Then a few days later I got THE call; they wanted me! My professional career was about to begin! And in what a fashion! As I look at pictures in my hallway, me meeting the Queen Mother, Queen Elizabeth and her husband and sister backstage at the Drury Lane, former President Truman and his wife back-

stage in Missouri, memories of Satchmo in the front row in Louisiana, President Johnson backstage in Texas, Liberace and Dan Duryea at parties, Gower Champion and Mary Martin dancing after opening night in London. I still marvel at my good fortune."
—JUDITH DRAKE

CHAPTER 4

Work—What's Your Plan?

Just as the route into your career is singular, your work once you get there is all you. As in your life, your career path will take unexpected twists and turns, and you will stumble upon surprising roadblocks despite your clearest intentions and most careful planning. Whether you approach your career with specific goals and choose to be selective about the jobs you take, or accept whatever turns up to pay your bills, one thing is for sure, you have to be prepared for uncertainty.

There is no getting around the whimsy and unpredictability of show business. No matter how much you have planned, you have to be willing to revise or change the plan. Sometimes the unpredictability can be a wonderful surprise. Things might happen faster or more easily than you anticipated. Or, perhaps it isn't moving as quickly as you thought nor going in the direction you had hoped. Be flexible and ready to make adjustments. Plans are good, as long as you are willing to be flexible.

Even if you are fortunate enough to be working fairly steadily, you will, at various times, agonize over career decisions. Should you commit to the potentially multi-season contract for a syndicated kid's show? Should you do the heavy rotation/high-paying hemorrhoid commercial? Should you take the regional theatre tour that keeps you on the road all year? Are you willing to take off your clothes for an iffy indie film? Wherever you are in your career—top of the heap, the middle or the bottom—chances are, you will frequently be conflicted over what step is the right decision at any given time.

Listen to opinions and feedback, but hit the "Edit" button and use only what feels right for you. We again remind you that you are the only one whose feelings really matter, and you are the one who has to live with your decision. Remember why you began this career and what unique individuality you have to offer a series, play or film. And respect yourself enough to think about what the series, play, or, film has to offer you.

In the long run, the most important element of your decision will be how true to yourself you remained. You will make mistakes of course, and you will learn from them and over time, have a better sense of what is right for you and how your decision impacts your reputation as an actor. Again, stay open and be flexible, but always grounded.

Typecasting, The Casting Couch, and The Magic of "NO"

DEBBIE: I wanted to be a star, plain and simple. It was my dream since the age of five to be an actress. That dream was in my heart since I was very young, and I just always believed I was special. Back in Kansas, I had no idea that there was anything but a star. Being an actress and acting meant you had to be a star. And of course I wanted an Oscar.

I practiced my speeches in the bathroom mirror in Kansas. What can I say? I was young and determined. Later I thought being a star would provide me with the freedom to do all the roles I wanted and turn down what I didn't. It would give me more control and power and recognition. But now I realize it is all relative. I knew where I wanted to end up, but the reality was I just wanted to work and was so very happy when someone said, "Yes" and hired me.

I had big dreams, but in the end I wanted to work and support myself as an actress. I was also raised to believe everything happens for the best. So I trusted that if I did this or that and conducted myself professionally the talent would win out, and my dream would come true. I didn't quite get to where I wanted, but in retrospect I came a long way from the teenage girl in Kansas. I always made a living and pretty much did it my way.

MOLLY: I had no master plan. I didn't think I was "enough" of an actress to do theatre, and I didn't have the ego or belief in my "artistry" to imagine a film career. I did figure I could probably handle TV, so I started just trying to get commercials. When that seemed to pan out, I took the great leap to Movies of the Week, and with a couple of tiny roles under my belt, I headed to Los Angeles for pilot season—and never returned.

Looking back, if I'd had a stronger sense of myself, I would've made different career moves, I'm sure, but as it was, I took a very passive stance and pretty much did what I was told to. For the most part, it worked out fine, but there are certainly roles I regret having agreed to audition for, knowing how viscerally uncomfortable I was doing them.

DEBBIE: It's like a golf game. Golf is a one-person game. You have to concentrate on your game and doing the best you can. You cannot let the other player's game affect you. We all have our own game to play. Sometimes we win, and sometimes we lose, and sometimes we just work–all in our own way. You have to struggle and try really hard not to worry about the end result. And, you must remember to not compare yourself to anyone else! It is hard to do that when directors, agents, casting directors and others invariably want to call you, "The Next XX," "Another XX," or "XX's sister." I was thought of as a Georgia Engel, Goldie Hawn or Diane Keaton.

MOLLY: Oh, I was Jane Fonda all the way. Even she mentioned the resemblance! It's partly a sort of shorthand, but it does tend to squeeze you into a specific box.

DEBBIE: Like a prototype. It makes it very hard to hang on to your own identity and how you see your career. I guess you could say it is flattering, but I actually hated it. I wanted to scream, "No! I am not that. I'm a Debbie Zipp type. I'm good enough being me."

I actually found out once that a casting director was looking for a "Debbie Zipp type" when casting a TV commercial. It was so flattering—though they didn't give me an audition.

MOLLY: As much as you hate hearing this, you need to find the deeper meaning. You just have to say, "Okay, they mean I'm quirky and good with comedy." You have to try not to take it personally and stand proud in your own talent and persona.

DEBBIE: Oh absolutely. It took a while, but I found my way to put a positive spin on it. Another struggle was busting out of the comedy genre "box." In college 99 percent of the stage roles I was cast in were dramatic. You can't get more serious than *The Lower Depths* or *The Good Woman of Szechuan*. It was a surprise to me when my first job was the lead comedic character in a TV pilot. From then on I was mostly doing the comedic ingénue. It took a big shift in my thinking.

MOLLY: Funny, my situation was opposite. Jane Fonda equaled drama, so I spent years trying to break into sit-coms, which is where I wanted to be all along. I think we all basically wanted the opportunity to do both, partly for the experience but also in hopes that showing versatility would open up and extend our careers.

DEBBIE: And let's not forget the other big minimizer: our physical appearance. I was up for parts all the time where they wanted big boobs, so most of the time I didn't get the job. Anyway, once they wanted me bad enough for a part for which I clearly didn't have those physical attributes, so they built a big set of boobs to attach to me, complete with the appropriate shading and all. And it looked real. I was the dumb buxom blonde for once.

You just never know!

MOLLY: Hey, I got my SAG card doing a Playtex bra commercial, so I know my career hinged on my "attributes"! The point is, though that you learn how to adapt to the limitations imposed on you and pick your battles to push the envelope.

DEBBIE: Once, a producer wanted me to be nude in a commercial because I was supposed to be in the shower using this new soap. Now of course none of my private parts were going to be shown on TV, but I still had to shoot nude. I have no problem with other people doing nude scenes, but I was just not comfortable doing it so I said "No."

My agent was begging me to say "Yes." It was scheduled to air prime time after all. However, I was willing to give up all the money I would make in residuals and stood my ground. It just wasn't me. My husband always said to me "If they want you bad enough, they'll make it work with you." Well, guess what? They wanted me bad enough, so they made a flesh tone colored bikini that the camera could work around, and one in which I was comfortable. And so, I did commercial—on my terms.

MOLLY: That brings to mind the magic of "NO." It's a generalization, but one with some legs, that the more you say "No," the harder they try to win you. I read for a pilot I thought was pretty mediocre and had way too many "dick jokes" for my taste.

It was early in pilot season, and having just come off two long-running series, I felt okay waiting for something I liked better. So, when they called to make a test deal, I declined. They kept coming back to my agents trying to change my mind because the star of the show wanted me, but I stuck to my guns.

Ultimately, at the end of the season having lost out on another pilot I wanted, I agreed to do the show for more money than they'd originally offered. I'm not sure I could've played hard to get like that had it been a project I loved, or if I'd really needed the money, but I've heard many times and many ways, that the less you need them, the more they want you. Again, just try to get it done, your way.

DEBBIE: Doing it "my way" and performing the character the way I wanted was always my goal—no matter what medium. But of course, there is the director.

Most of the time directors are great and sometimes, even an inspiration to work with. But there are those directors who aren't the best communicators, or who make your life difficult because of their massive egos.

I always made sure I knew the lines backwards and forwards. All the data had to be in the computer so I was free to play and experiment, or able to adjust to any environment I found myself in. It was always the first thing I did for the role and myself.

When you are being paid to deliver, you can't be worrying about extra stuff like remembering lines. You have to be able to concentrate and focus on what the director or producer wants from you, and still try to make yourself happy. It doesn't always happen but if you can do that—if you can please yourself and the producers—it's sheer heaven.

MOLLY: For the most part, my experience has been in television, and I've found that directors tend to be good at working with the actors, or good at the technical aspects—but rarely both. So, I have felt largely on my own once it came to my performance. Other than blocking my moves, I got very little actual direction; at least not what I'd imagined direction would be. I don't in any way mean to minimize the contribution of directors in general, but especially in TV, it's the writer-producers and the stars that run the show.

Sometimes that means you'll get an abundance of attention from the director when you guest-star, because you're all he or she has any power over. Sometimes they'll feel compelled to say something for appearance's sake that you have to just agree with and then go about your business pretending it was what they suggested.

Again, no disrespect intended because God knows, in my mind, nothing would be more frightening than to be put in charge of a set—well maybe air traffic control. I came into the business with some old-movie idea about how involved directors would be with an actor's performance that has only infrequently played out in real life.

The point is, be prepared to be on your own once the camera rolls.

DEBBIE: I had the privilege of doing an *LA Law* television episode, and with a friend who was directing. Of course I was terrified I would embarrass my friend. So there was an added burden on the set; the pressure was on. As a guest star, or a co-star, you do not get rehearsals or a read-through before the day on the set. You are going in cold turkey.

My scene pretty much required me to cry from the get-go, which was okay I just used my fear of failing and the stress of not disappointing anyone, and some preparation, to come up with the goods. After the director asked for a couple of angles, I was very pleased with my performance and thought the pressure was off. I was sure I could relax a bit while they shot the other six or so in the scene. Well, that was not the case. Much to my surprise, they would do an angle or two on someone else and then come back to me for another angle on the same crying dialogue. "I have to do it again," I thought? I had to hurry up and get to that point of emotional readiness again. Somehow I did it.

This is how it went for more than eight hours that day. With a lunch break of course. I drew upon every acting technique or trick I could; I used every tear-inducing sense memory I could. I got to the point where I had to use the old "dead puppies" visualization to cry over and over again. Phew! If you are a regular on a series or a consistent character in a film, you are more at ease and relaxed in the first place, and you are afforded more time to prepare, which helps you connect to your emotions easier.

When you are a guest star and you are not a celebrity, you don't have the luxury of time or comfort. I was lucky in this case. My friend was a wonderful director who had been an actor himself and understood what an actor needed to give him the performance he wanted. You don't always get that, so you have to have as many tools available as possible, and you have to keep using them when you are not working so you can more easily access them to deliver a good performance even when the circumstances are not ideal.

MOLLY: I agree. It was a big surprise to find stars who would do the master and their own close-ups and then leave the set before the camera turned around on me. TV acting requires you to have the goods instantaneously and without a lot of support much of the time.

Despite the endless drudgery of waiting for sets to be lit and ready, the actual acting work goes very quickly. Budgets demand speed. It's really not conducive to working as you do in class or on stage. You don't have the time to prepare or "get yourself there," so you learn to develop a sort of short hand and some tricks along the way which often make you feel you aren't staying true to your higher artistry, also known as being a hack.

It's extremely hard not to be result-oriented on a set. But that's the yin-yang of professional acting. You balance your technique and craft with the exigencies of the medium and hope you can watch the finished product without wincing.

DEBBIE: Of course doing theatre is different, at least for me. You have had rehearsals and collaboration and you have so much more control.

I did my best work on stage.

I wish I could have seen myself somehow performing on stage. I think there would have been a lot less wincing. But there are directors, writers and producers there as well, and you have to be a professional and treat them with respect in the majority of circumstances. In conducting your career and your craft you have to balance what is expected of you and what you are comfortable with and who you are in the context of show business. It is no easy feat.

MOLLY: What you are comfortable with is key, which brings me to a subject we've been encouraged to include since we are talking to newcomers: sex in the workplace.

DEBBIE: The bottom line here is that it's just like every other decision you make about how to conduct your career. The choice to blur the professional and personal lines is all up to the individual—but it CAN be a slippery slope. You really have to question your own motives and understand what the trade-off is. There's no all-inclusive right answer to how to respond to advances made at work or in auditions.

MOLLY: However, an actor should never fear standing up and refusing any sexual advances no matter how subtle. If your gut instinct tells you it is inappropriate or the actions of someone else make you uncomfortable or fearful, speak up to a stage manager, union representative, agent or fellow cast member. There were no sexual harassment laws on the books when we were young actors, but there are now.

I do think there is a heightened awareness now because of the threat of sexual harassment lawsuits, so most people in a position of power these days conduct themselves much more carefully. Just know that sacrificing your integrity and self-worth is never a good career move.

DEBBIE: At the end of the day, the career decisions with which we come face-to-face, are ours to make. Stay strong! Stay true to who you are, and, trust our own inner voice—because it will give an advantage in conducting your career.

Insight and Sage Advice from Well-Seasoned Actors

"Trust your instinct. We all have an ability to notice little signs in life that tell us what is right for us. And many times we ignore them or let others tell us that we should ignore them. Will we all make mistakes? Of course but they will be your mistakes, and you will learn from them. Your gut is a good truth machine, both in life as a whole and in your artistic work." **—JEANNE HART-MAN**

"I read once that Jung had a sign over his study door that read, 'THIS IS MY WAY. WHAT IS YOUR WAY? THERE IS NO ONE WAY.' As I am producing, directing and choreographing nowadays more than acting, I find that the actors I hire are the ones that are the most authentic; they ring true to their own tone. And, of course, they are the ones who enjoy what they are doing the most." **—MURPHY CROSS**

"I think it's important for actors just coming into the business, no matter what their age, to know that there is a way to pursue this business with kindness, focus and commitment. It doesn't have to be nasty competition. One of my best friends in the world, Susie Duff, is my 'fiercest competitor,' as she puts it. All I know is, that if I don't get the job, I want her to get the job because somebody is going to get the job, so it might as well be one of us." —**MAGGIE EGAN-CUMMINGS**

"The single most important thing is attitude. Attitude monitors talent. And the thing that made the difference for me more than anything else was learning and accepting my casting. Most of us are character actors, and it can be a tough pill to swallow. But once I accepted myself and my place in the world I started working and have never looked back. I believe that slow and steady winds the race. I used to think I was a sprinter, but now I've discovered I'm a long distance runner. Hi diddle-de-de, an actor's life for me!" —**BETH GRANT**

"Actors often bristle at being typecast. In a Master's acting class, I witnessed the teacher, Milton Katseles, take a moderately well-known actor to task for complaining about it and the fact that it was keeping him from being considered for other kinds of roles. 'Maybe, you should stop resisting being typecast and learn how to do it better,' he said. 'Becoming known for doing something exceptionally well can make you a star. And once you're a star they'll let you play anything.' Then he turned to the rest of us and exclaimed, 'So if you don't have a 'type,' you'd better get one!'" —**MARIANN AALDA**

"You've heard it before but I'll say it again: 'Let YOUR Light SHINE!' You have a unique and special individual presence that is yours and yours alone. Embrace you, empower you, embody YOU always!" Silly story, but a good point. So, I had this frizzy curly hair that I tried and tried to straighten, so I would look like everyone else. For years I spent hours preparing my hair for an audition, chemically dependent on hair straightening products, and contributing to feelings of self-consciousness and insecurity. Then, once I booked a job, I had anxiety about where it would shoot and if it happened to be near a beach or humid area, OMG!

This was really terrifying for me. I actually believed my hair made the difference in getting a job or doing a job well. I could go on and on about this and write an entire book on this subject alone. I even lost a part to Amy Irving because they liked her 'curly' hair and I still didn't get the message. The irony, and the point here, is that when I finally decided to embrace my hair and its 'uniqueness,' it ended up being a calling card for me. What I thought was a curse, was truly a blessing, when I chose to see it that way, I'm just sayin!" —SHERRY HURSEY

"I was doing a new play in New York City at an off-Broadway theatre. At one of the rehearsals the director told me to bang my fist on the table before saying my next line. I resisted, saying that it didn't make sense to me to bang my fist on the table for no apparent reason. 'Just do it,' he insisted. So I did. Out poured a flood of tears and deep anger that I didn't even know was there. I never resisted after that. Always be willing to play. Allow yourself to be surprised." —ANNE MARIE HOWARD

"It always seemed to me that it was a good idea to say yes to any and all opportunities to act. Well, okay, not porn. Not that anyone asked me to do porn. But I digress. Anyway, when I got the chance to do a looping job (background voices for movies and TV shows), I knew that I had found my acting niche. It was so much fun! Challenging, in that one has to be able to do all kinds of voices and accents and turn them on at a moment's notice. But I got to use all my acting tools and get paid union bucks and have the personal satisfaction of helping a scene come alive on screen." —DORIS HESS

"Voiceover is an art form unto itself. After years working in films, television, commercials and stage I found something that could support my acting 'habit' THAT I LOVED. The biggest plus, was that no matter what age I was chronologically, I could voice every race, age and gender necessary for a role. *The Simpsons*; Mrs. Hibbert; Sanja (Apu's wife—all the old women in the old folks home with grandpa); as well as Dolph and Richard

(Bart's friends), are just a few examples of the race and age challenge that I encountered." —**MAGGIE ROSWELL**

"Actor Richard Greene shared this pearl of wisdom with me, passed down to him by way of generations of actors, when he came to see a show I had co-written and was co-starring in. 'You've got something here that no one can take away from you,' he said. 'So when no one else is hiring you, you can always hire yourself. Every actor needs his own pushcart.' Lena Dunham, the 27 year old writer-creator and star of the hit HBO series *Girls*, though not a conventional Hollywood beauty, was able to 'show em something else.' She made a pushcart from her skill as writer and built a cog capable of tapping into the growing-pains angst of her peer group of young adults—which also happens to be the commercial brass ring to most advertisers. The lesson to be learned here is that every actor who wants to go the distance needs to be aware of what lane she belongs in, what assets she can draw on from her wheelhouse, when it's time to change lanes, and how to build a pushcart that, when it comes to the wheels of commerce, can turn, baby, turn!" —**MARIANN AALDA**

"It's okay to say NO without an explanation. This is great advice for women. Many times we have been taught to 'be nice' and to 'fix it for everyone else.' That is wonderful for people who deserve your focus and kindness but you don't have to do that for everyone. I think any young woman who decides to become an actress or singer or dancer should learn how to stand firm on her beliefs and morals. And if she needs to say 'NO,' she doesn't have to explain it to the person who wants her to do something that she doesn't want to do. Quite frankly there are a lot of bullies in the world and they will push you even after you have said 'NO.' This might be good for every young woman to learn but especially if you want to be in show business." —**JEANNE HARTMAN**

"You make your own decisions; make your own way; open your own doors." —**IONA MORRIS**

CHAPTER 5

You—"The Product"

At some point you begin to look at the jobs you're getting as more than a series of miraculous flukes and realize you are beginning a career—you are becoming a career actor.

A career requires responsibility to more than the continued development and nurturing of your artistry. Sure, talent matters, but every successful actor will tell you how many other actors in their acting classes who never "made it" had more of a gift for acting than he or she did—and that it was the drive to succeed and the luck factor that made the difference.

Luck you can only hope for, but ambition and business smarts you can absolutely supply for yourself. Consider yourself a product and devote a certain amount of energy to the promotion, protection and management of the "You" commodity.

Mercifully, there are agents, managers, PR firms, unions, accountants and lawyers to handle much of the heavy lifting, but no one cares as much about your career, money and quality of life as you do. Many actors say, "I'm an artist, not a business person," but that is a common mistake. Running your career like a business, right from the get-go, can make all the difference in the amount of control you have over your career and its longevity.

You Are an Artist—But Your Career is a Business

DEBBIE: Looking for work, or "Lerking" as I call it, is the main focus of your business. The work is in getting the audition and the job and everything that encompasses that. You can't sit around eating bonbons waiting for the phone to ring. You have to be proactive between auditions.

MOLLY: Managing all the time between jobs is a talent, too. You can't allow yourself to fall too far out of the loop, so you need to invent work-related tasks and activities to sustain your momentum. Plays, workshops, classes, physical exercise, networking—whatever keeps you in a state of preparedness for the invariably last-minute audition.

DEBBIE: Yes, you must always stay ready. You never know when that amazing opportunity could present itself. Even though it may not come naturally to you as an artist, you have to be willing to push yourself to meet people, to make connections and develop professional relationships, network, utilize social media and whatever other tools that are available to get your name and face out there on a consistent basis.

Explore and exploit any advantage to get to the place you need to be, to get an agent or get an audition. Of course methods will keep changing, but it is certainly a part of the acting game that you need to be good at.

MOLLY: Over all, it's important to remember that you are running a business. On the upside, the start-up costs are pretty minimal: headshots and acting workshop fees aren't much in the small business world. The more you treat your career as a profession, the better. Be professional. Show up prepared, on time and knowing as much as possible about the project and or the people in charge. And give the best performance you have in you at that moment.

Insight and Sage Advice from Well-Seasoned Actors

"I wish I knew that as an actress I also needed business skills."
—PAT LENTZ

"Find out all you can about the business. What's working today? Study theatre, film and television. Know who's done what in the genres you like. Writers, directors, casting agents, actors,

and so on. Watch and study the work in the industry. Yes, study."
—**ROBIN POLK**

"Make no mistake, show biz is definitely a game and you get points for things like: talent, great personality, good looks, being married to the producer, and so on. But the thing to remember is that the rules of the game and the things you get points for are constantly changing, so you have to be alert because nobody's gonna send out a memo. When you notice that a lot of 'unconventional' looking girls are getting hired and you're in the 'quirky' category, get into high gear and get in a play and send out postcards. Do whatever you need to do to make sure you get noticed. Strike while the iron is hot because in the blink of an eye the rules are gonna change again." —**MARIANN AALDA**

"You are a product. Brand yourself and market your product well. Do at least one thing every day to move your acting career forward." —**ANNE MARIE HOWARD**

"In the early days of my career I had a work buddy. She and I would talk every day and tell each other five things each would do for our careers. It was all just footwork and the five things could be simple like write a thank you note, read Variety, go to class, and rehearse a scene. It was so helpful. Action, action, action! The results are never up to us, but we can stay in action, taking steps to move forward." —**BETH GRANT**

"This is indeed a business. Treat it as one. Keep track of jobs and list details such as dates, director, casting agent, payments, residuals and so on. This can all be kept in a simple notebook with each page representing a job. Keep a daily planner and know your ratio of auditions to bookings. These are all clues. Note your wardrobe on auditions. What is working, what isn't? And, most importantly, provide your Agent/Manager with the tools he or she needs to promote you. And, thank them. Always."
—**SUE MULLEN**

"I am certain a large part of my success is due to the fact that I approach my career as a business. My career goals guided all my career decisions: take classes, invest my money, write thank you notes, always be prepared, go to the wrap party, don't gossip, it's not about me, audition for myself, be professional, know my rights, understand my unions, and so much more."
—**MARIANNE MUELLERLEILE**

"I don't think, in the beginning, that I DID approach it as a business. It almost seems counter-intuitive. I went into the "business" of acting, as a living, not from any practical, or monetary (I wanted to be famous, but who doesn't?) position, but from the conceit that I HAD to do this, had to act. I will specify, at this point, that acting, for me, was in the sacred halls of THEATRE, not in film, or, God forbid, television. I have since revised that lofty, somewhat psuedo-intellectual, arrogant position. I made more money in my years of film and television, (fewer jobs, MUCH less time) than in the whole of my theatrical career. (I made more in two years on *The Guiding Light* than in all the Desdemonas, Roxannes, and Molly Browns or Heddas combined). But the need to tell a story, to narrate a character's journey, was tantamount to anything else. It remains true to this day. My advice to young women wanting to start out as actresses is to 1) go to school, and learn how to do it; 2) study other things as well, and learn about life and its impulses, and 3) see and discover if there is anything else that compels or drives or interests you. Search for it!" —**DEBORAH MAY**

"This is a very emotional, creative career and because of that, one cannot rely solely on the heart and "feelings" in making decisions about your career. As we all know, emotions can run you, but in business that is absolutely the wrong thing to have happen. Learning the business of the entertainment business allows you to stay in control (somewhat), of your career. It allows you to make decisions on which direction to go, when your emotions might push you in a direction that does not assist your goals. You can get trapped in people liking you, relationships, desires that are not supportive of where you are trying to go. When you come to this from a business point of view, you have a longer life span and I think reach greater heights." —**IONA MORRIS**

CHAPTER 6

Manage Your Money—or You'll Be a "Starving Artist"

It's no coincidence that the most common reaction potential actors get to their choice of profession is horror and derision. We know all too well there is no job security in this line of work, and even successful careers include long stretches of unemployment. All the statistics show that some 92 percent of actors are out of work at one time, and the same 8 percent or so are the ones who work continuously. For a woman, the picture is even more bleak.

Despite being 50 percent of the population, only 44 percent of all major roles are female characters, and the minor role percentages are similar. (You'll find some resources in Appendix C in the back of this book to support these claims and to further your understanding.)

Uncertainty is the norm, and forced retirement comes early—especially for women. When 63 percent of the roles available to women go to 20 and 30 year-olds, the obsession with youth in all areas of the media and society is directly tied to the loss of opportunities as an actress ages.

It holds true for men as well, but they have a much longer shelf life. So, it is highly likely an actress will be semi-retired by the age of 45. Athletes and gorgeous leading women, especially, fall prey to the statute of peak-performance limitations. Age will inevitably influence your hot looks, so if they are your primary calling card, take advantage while you can, but know it won't last forever.

What is harder to understand is that the same rules apply to the "second banana." What difference could a few wrinkles make on the best friend or mom character? Well, as it turns out, it's a big difference. In TV-land, teenagers—often played by 20-some-things—have 25-30 year-old looking mothers and 40-some-things are sometimes grannies! So, while you may have had quite a bit of success in your 20's and 30's, it can be virtually over when you reach 40.

Bottom line: be scrupulous about your finances if you want to preserve your sanity, the ability to say "no" when you want to, and your freedom to stay in the profession you chose.

Planning for a Rainy Day—or Year!

DEBBIE: We know all too well there is no job security in this line of work. Even major stars have huge stretches when they are not working. However, they have a pile of money to see them through-or do they?

MOLLY: Not every actor who has "made it" with a series or a film career has done a good job handling their finances.

DEBBIE: You just have to save, save, save. I had a friend who was a regular on a series for many, many years. The friend wasn't the star and didn't command a huge salary but made A LOT of money. A few years later the friend was calling my husband and asking for a loan.

You need to save whenever you can, not only for your survival during dry spells but so you can turn down jobs you hate. I called it "The Go to Hell Fund."

MOLLY: Well, I did not plan financially with the expectation of being unable to work more than once a year from ages 41-49. And figuring out a new revenue source at 41 with no other employment history or business skills than being a working actress is no picnic.

DEBBIE: Oh yes, the ageism thing. It is brutal. After you reach a certain point and age you think you will at least continue to earn a livable wage. It is such a shock when you can't. I didn't plan for that.

MOLLY: Luckily for me, my career was partially resuscitated by a fluky, last-minute substitution in a film that turned into one of the major film franchises of the '90s.

DEBBIE: I remember that *American Pie* came out of nowhere. So wonderful!

MOLLY: But before that, I was reduced to scrambling for odd jobs, crying a lot and taking in roommates for a substantial part of my 40's. Still, I will be the first to tell you that saving for a very early retirement is critical. This is especially true for women embarking on an acting career, regardless of when she begins her career.

DEBBIE: Of course in the beginning of the career you have nothing. You have to be smart and make sacrifices. Just because you possess everything it takes to be a success, it does not guarantee you will get work. You will be freer in pursuit of your dream if you know there will be a roof over your head and food in the fridge with or without that acting job.

MOLLY: Desperation shows no matter how hard you try to hide it, especially in auditions or meetings.

DEBBIE: So you need to adopt the attitude that anything legal you do to pay the bills and support your "habit," as I like to refer to it, i.e. to support your dream as an actor, is part of the game.

When you look at the side jobs or the less than rewarding acting jobs like TV commercials as a means of financing your dream it is a lot easier to deal with. Doing on-camera TV commercials was my way of supporting my TV and Film career. I was lucky. I never had to have a side job outside of acting once I got my first commercial. Before that, well, I already mentioned the file clerking, the singing waitress gig, but oh dear, I forgot I was a maid for a couple of weeks at a famous rock band's house. I worked at Jack in the Box for a week and couldn't make the milkshakes right and dropped the tomato-cutter and then tried to catch it and cut one of my hands. I was a magician's assistant one night and blew the trick for him, so I wonder why I forgot those disasters?

It was clear to me I wasn't good at anything but acting. Anyway, I did what I had to do to survive until I got that first on-camera commercial. Then I was off and running and commercials became my day job, so to speak. Commercials and those residuals paved the way for me to pay the bills for my entire career. The income from that provided me peace of mind and allowed me to be flexible in my decisions with regards to my television and film role selections. Of course times change and each actress is different. What works for one might not work for the other.

MOLLY: What is really interesting is that these days, the working world in general seems to be mirroring the working life of an actor. Most actors have had to make peace with the notion that they will need to hold down more than one job in order to finance their acting dream. Now, almost everyone must supplement their income no matter what their field.

DEBBIE: So, perhaps, for once, actors might be better prepared for "real life" than those who are considered more practical for having chosen reliable and stable professions.

Insight and Sage Advice from Well-Seasoned Actors

"Don't assume that other people will take care of your money better than you. Certainly get help or advice, but you keep your eye on it. Sign your own checks and look at your statements, no matter how busy you get or how much money you make. Put some of it away because there will be times when you will need it." —**JEANNE HARTMAN**

"When I moved from Iowa to New York City to become an actress, I worked as a waitress until I didn't have to anymore. The money I made was wisely invested in my career. The job was flexible and my manager was supportive. He always made sure I could go to my auditions, even if it meant being short a waiter. Find a way to make ends meet that supports you fully." —**ANNE MARIE HOWARD**

"Understand and control your own finances. I wish I would have known more about finances. My biggest mistake was not buying a house. I was making very good money and renting wonderful apartments and even for a few years rented a great view home in the Hollywood Hills. I kept thinking I should wait to buy my dream home once I got on a series that ran for a few years. I never got one that went past 13 weeks! But if I had bought a modest home back in the early '80s I would be way ahead of the game. I am so grateful that I eventually bought a townhouse once my career began to slow down. And I count my blessings for finally making that decision. Also, I lost nearly $100,000 in a bad investment. I trusted a business manager who was not a crook at all, and believed he was making a good choice. But still, I know now you never put all your eggs in one basket. Also I was incorporated. That did not accomplish much more than simply generating very high monthly bills to accountants. I see other people who I am sure didn't make as much money having the home with the white picket fence. So take it from me: invest your money very carefully. And buy a home." —**TERESA GANZEL**

"The quote I always tell folks is when an actress confronted me and said 'I NEVER do commercials. I AM AN ACTRESS, I only do theater and film.' My response was 'Really? They give me money to support my acting career.'" —**MAGGIE ROSWELL**

"Always keep a side-job or day-job unless you're wildly wealthy and maybe even then. One of the best places for character study is at a job where you see the same fellow employees on a regular basis. It's also a place to have a sense of camaraderie that is usually without competition because fellow workers often want you to succeed at the 'acting thing.' It's great to be able to pay the bills!" —**ROBIN POLK**

"Go to a used bookstore and get a Casserole Cookbook; the recipes are cheap and easy to make and last days." —JUDITH DRAKE

CHAPTER 7

Agents: You Pretty Much Can't Live Without Them

In an ideal world, your relationship with an agent would be a long-term affair. He or she would discover you, formulate a career strategy, be by your side to advise every move, soothe you through the disappointments, and celebrate your successes. For the most part, that is a fantasy.

An agent is licensed by the state as an employment agency, which gives you the essence of their role. They seek out work opportunities for you, provide access to auditions, and when you secure a part, they negotiate the terms of your employment, from salary to various perks like dressing room size. The degree to which they offer support and counsel varies, but the bottom line is that you can't work without an agent.

In the beginning, of course, you are consumed with finding an agent, any agent, to represent you. While we are not in the specific "how-to" business here, suffice it to say there are many, many avenues to connecting with representation. Appearances in plays and low-budget indie films through open auditions that are listed in trade magazines are great calling cards. Casting workshops, classes and friend referrals are also effective.

Keep in mind that agencies need new talent all the time. They are not doing you a favor by signing you; they wouldn't exist without artists to promote. It's true you can't have a career without them, but they are mainly facilitators. Don't expect an agency to create a career for you.

Managing the Relationship with Your Agent

DEBBIE: It is very hard for an actor to embrace the business side of an artistic career. An agent is so vital to having any kind of acting career, let alone a successful one.

It is hard to know sometimes how to deal with them. How much hands-on guidance should you ask for or expect? How much personal attention do you legitimately need from them? I was not good at this at all. If I had been truthful about what I wanted and expected, and looked at it in a more business-like manner instead of as a grateful actress, who knows what I might have accomplished.

MOLLY: Well, that is the trick isn't it? It is hard to remember that agents work for us. We are not working for them.

DEBBIE: Somehow as actresses we have to make friends with the fact that we are the boss of the agent, and the agent is an employee. I mean we are paying them a percentage when we work. I have to confess I never acquired that attitude, and I think it hurt me in the long run. The pervasive attitude in Hollywood is that the actor is never in control.

MOLLY: Plus you have to jump through so many hoops to get an agent, and you can't possibly have a career without one.

DEBBIE: Unless you are such a big star that you just need a manager and a lawyer to negotiate deals.

MOLLY: But if you aren't, it is virtually impossible to get an audition without one.

DEBBIE: And, it painful if an agent drops you. Being dropped by an agent made me feel like I had been set out to sea on a raft with no sail or oars. So with that in the back of my mind, I was afraid to bother agents because I was always so afraid I would be dropped as a client. It only happened once or twice, but it colored the way I dealt with my agents.

MOLLY: Don't run a business from a place of fear. I had to overcome my timidity and fire an agent. Though I've had wonderful agents over the years—and in one case, my agent single-handedly revived my career. I also had an agent who got a call to test me for a series who, according to that producer, tried to push another of his better-known clients instead of me because he could get more money for her. That was unacceptable. I mean, they wanted ME, and my agent was working against me. But, I got the series anyway in spite of him.

DEBBIE: It is definitely easier shopping for an agent when you are employed. It is so much easier if you are in the wonderful position to move up the ladder from a less-well-connected agent, or let's just say someone who isn't doing a good job for you, to better-positioned representation.

MOLLY: Well yes, but it is also pure foolishness to believe that who your agent is will determine how successful you are. I wish aspiring actors could see how incessant agency-hopping to find the magic bullet agent could backfire later when jobs become scarcer and clients are being dropped for their age.

DEBBIE: Absolutely. The loyalty that might have been fostered by staying with them and developing a stronger relationship with a lesser-known agent can stand you in very good stead when times are lean and opportunities fewer.

Also, when choosing an agent you absolutely have to look at their connections, and what they've done for other clients. You have to feel in your gut that they are easy to communicate with and they really truly believe in you and your talent and will work their heart out for you. You must sense that the agent is hungry for you to work. Those are very important factors as well. Otherwise the phone won't ring with auditions.

MOLLY: Again, you can't rely on an agent to do all the work.

Insight and Sage Advice from
Well-Seasoned Actors

"Don't be afraid to change agents. Remember, your agent is not your mother or father figure; he or she is a business partner, and need to treat you as an equal in this business endeavor and just like you should do the same to them. Demand it graciously and don't apologize. Nobody is doing you a favor."
—CLAUDETTE SUTHERLAND

"Find one that has integrity, believes in your talent, is not out to change you, but to enhance who you already are—someone who has a vision for you that supports what yours is for yourself. Remember, this is a business. Yes, you want to find someone who you resonate with on a personal level, but you also want to find someone who will go out and fight for you. Do not allow an agent to put you down, to be critical of who you are. You need someone who supports you and is going to be in your corner. Do not be afraid to leave an agent, but my advice is to have a new one before you leave the one you are with. The reason why I say do not be afraid to leave your agent because sometimes it is just not working. You may have started out well with each other, and then things are not going as well as they had in the beginning. 'No harm no foul.' When that happens, graciously depart. Always keep your relationships intact, if you can. Your job is to remain honorable in the face of what is difficult, and that is not always easy. Don't worry, you will make mistakes, and this is good, because mistakes are there for you to learn from. Do not let anything bring you down. Keep your head up and keep your goal in sight." —IONA MORRIS

"Find your team and know who is REALLY on your team. I talk a lot about your team to young actresses, and actors too. Your team should have these qualities. Hopefully some of your team will be people who knew you before you make it big. They should be people who have loyalty and an honest integrity. They should be people who will tell you the truth even when you don't want to hear it and even when all the 'Yes' people in the world are leading you astray. Now, some of your team will be people who you meet after you become well-known, but hopefully by then you will be able to recognize who are people that have your back and are reaally on your side. Also these friends need to be okay that there will be times that no one will notice them because you are the famous one or the one on stage that night." —**JEANNE HARTMAN**

CHAPTER 8

Auditions: How Can I Get The Job?

Auditions are an entirely different animal than performing a role on stage, TV, or film. You still need to use all the same techniques and tools those venues require, but under highly-anxious, often awkward circumstances that are largely out of your control.

The trick is to narrow your focus on the few elements you can control. Learning the specific procedures for the various types of auditions will give you some degree of sure-footedness. For example, commercials differ from TV and film, and reading for producers differs from pre-reading for the casting director. Again, learn the protocol and follow it.

You will eventually learn this through experience, but prior to that there are many classes or workshops available to guide and prepare you for auditions in all media.

The single most important boon to your confidence in auditioning is this fact: there is no right way to perform a role in an audition. The secret to a successful audition is knowing that producers and directors are looking for whoever walks in and takes the decision out of their hands. They want the character to present itself to them. You can't possibly know what the character looks like inside their minds, but you can come in with a clear, assured idea of your own that makes them comfortable handing over the reins to you.

Your individual take on the material and your professionalism in giving the best performance you possibly can IS in your control.

Sometimes Pepto Bismol and Auditions Go Hand In Hand

MOLLY: I wish I could get back the hours I spent trying to figure out what they were looking for and just focused on how I saw the roles.

DEBBIE: I wish I understood early on that they really want you to be right for the part so they can stop worrying about it.

MOLLY: Yes, as nerve-wracking as it is to feel judged, it's not actually an adversarial situation!

DEBBIE: I kind of learned that early in my career when I realized how much the feedback I got before a callback helped me. I had already been in to read for the producers for a TV pilot. They really liked me and were calling me back, but they told my agent that they thought I was too bubbly and not geeky enough for the role. So, when they gave me a second chance with that specific info, I made sure I walked in as the character they wanted and even when the scene was done and they were talking to me I still gave them the essence of that character. I wasn't taking any chances. I ended up going back many times and eventually got the job.

MOLLY: I also think it is important to bring something more into the audition room than just your work. I have always made a point of having an opening comment prepared, whether based on the material to be read, the latest news item, or something personal; anything somehow connected to the situation. It gives you a sense of control over the moment (however false that may actually be), and the casting people and producers get a sense of your personality outside the character you're playing—which may serve as a nice counterpoint to highlight the work you've put into your interpretation of the role. I don't mean you should take valuable time away from the audition itself by arriving with a monologue, just an off-hand remark that shows you have a brain and a personality will suffice.

DEBBIE: That's interesting. For me, it depended on the role and the emotional life of the role I was auditioning for—or basically, if I didn't have to begin the material from a place of deep emotion. When that was the case I liked to just say "hello" and get on with it because I'd been preparing to burst into tears right away or scream in anger in the lobby.

MOLLY: Good point.

DEBBIE: My husband had a lead recurring role as Grady on "Murder She Wrote." They were looking for someone to play his girlfriend and soon-to-be wife. They were looking at celebrities. My name came up with the producers and they knew me of course and knew I was good at comedy but didn't think I could handle the dramatic moments in the script.

MOLLY: There's typecasting rearing its ugly head.

DEBBIE: They granted me an audition. There is nothing worse than auditioning for friends. The scene I was given to audition with started out with me bursting into tears because the character I was playing had accidentally killed someone with a big frozen fish.

Sounds comedic to me. Oh brother! However, I did not want to chat or do anything but start the scene, because the scene started with me bursting into tears. I needed to be able to hold on to my preparation in the waiting room. Just boom. Walk in the room. Say hello and burst into tears.

Actually I was so nervous and terrified I would embarrass my husband—who had been on the show a few years, I actually took a Pepto Bismol tablet before-hand and all the terror of those real life emotions swelled up inside me and bursting into tears was no problem.

MOLLY: And you got the job?

DEBBIE: Oh yes. Thank goodness. But on the other end of the scale if the scene and type of character were comedic or less intense I would come in to the audition ready to chat a little using my wit and charm to energize my character and myself. I've just always liked to change with different audition scenarios.

MOLLY: As actors, part of the job in an audition is to read the room. Be prepared and ready to be open to whatever situation will present itself.

DEBBIE: You need to know yourself and what will work for you. What works for you, Molly, in an audition as you can see might not work for me.

MOLLY: And first and foremost, an actor is there to serve the written material.

I have unlimited respect for the art of writing, but at the end of most scenes, there is usually room for you to react to what's preceded, and I advise improvising a "tag" line of your own in keeping with the spirit of the character. It could just be a look, or it could be a riff off where the scene ended, but if it's done well, it shows a few things: that you get the character and are able to keep her alive even in the silences, and it also distinguishes your performance from the 20 other people who came in and delivered the script only as written.

Just be judicious and respectful of the writers.

DEBBIE: For me, again, we think just a tad differently. For me it depends if it is comedy or drama. Drama, I tend to just stop, take a moment and then say "Thank you." But I definitely see the importance and advantage of your way. Most important is to be conscious of setting yourself apart from the countless others reading for the same role. I've never been comfortable coming in with props, a good opening line, and so on. I just feel it makes me look like I'm trying too hard. So I never did it. I did have confidence that my interpretation and my persona would be different from the rest. But that is just me.

MOLLY: I just believe doing a "good job" with the scene is only part of the task. A memorable entrance, an appropriate prop, a funny bit as long as they are not labored and are organic to the proceedings, can help you stand out.

Whether or not you stand out well is all in the smartness and comfort of the tack you take.

DEBBIE: Absolutely! I agree that being comfortable in what you're doing is key. I went to a commercial workshop once when I wasn't booking and she gave, even though it was a commercial workshop, a lot of good general audition advice. Being comfortable with what you are doing is key. And so is your attitude. You need to walk in and remember it is your time and "You've been invited." Take stage, take control and make it your moment. If you have to restart, then do it.

Always remember you are welcome there because you have been invited in.

MOLLY: Yeah, I think the longer you do it you recognize the only thing you can walk out of the audition with is your own pride in how you handled it.

DEBBIE: Yes. That is all you've got; that you gave the performance and interpretation that you were hoping to give.

Insight and Sage Advice from Well-Seasoned Actors

"I had just gotten my first Equity job in New York, playing the lead in the original production of Lanford Wilson's *The Hot l Baltimore* at Circle in the Square. I was taking home $111 a week after taxes—and felt like I'd made it. No need to look for further employment.

My agent called me asking if I'd like to audition for some film called *All the President's Men* which would entail flying down to

D.C. 'No, sorry I can't. I'm in a show and don't have an understudy, Good-bye.'

I'm trying to imagine the incredulous look on my poor agent's face. She shortly called back and said, 'Now listen, Penny...' Cut to—I'm on a plane to D.C. on my show's dark day to read for whatever this little movie was. I mean, movies, please. I was a real actress. Let me add that today no one would get flown anywhere to audition for a tiny role, let alone an actress with no film credits.

Upon arriving the producer informed me I'd be reading with 'Dustin.' As in 'Hoffman.'

I was going to read for the only man I'd ever cut out pictures of and I was suddenly jelly. 'And you'll meet Bob,' he added. That would be 'Bob Redford.'

Arriving at the set I was led into director Alan Pakula's trailer with Mr. Hoffman. There was some small talk, none of it from me. We started reading the scene, which was very dry on paper. Dustin began improvising, which fortunately was something I was comfortable with—and luckily, my nerves happily served the scene. For those who don't know the film (it won Best Picture for 1976) it was about Watergate—which was my ace in the hole. As I shook hands and started to exit the trailer I turned to them and said, 'My dad's a Congressman. I know what this movie is about.'

And out. I'm convinced that's what clinched the role for me. Sharing something personal and relevant to the project. I didn't realize for years what a magical 'value add' that can be at an audition." —**PENNY PEYSER**

"Learn how to leave an audition feeling 'clean'—as if you have been present, responsive and simple. Resist auditioning for the job, audition for the sake of the audition." —**CLAUDETTE SUTHERLAND**

"Study, study, STUDY. If you sing, practice. If you act, take classes or workshops. If you dance, DANCE. Keep yourself sharp. There are a thousand of you out there wanting the same thing. And, take classes that stretch you. Take Improv classes, take an art class, take a cooking class. Expand your mind. You will be surprised what you think of in an audition because you took that Indian cooking class, or ran that 5K or started taking early morning walks on the beach to clear your mind before the beginning of your day." —**IONA MORRIS**

"Remember, the casting director, the producer and the director all want you to do well. They want you to solve their problem. No one is hoping you'll fall on your face, except the other actors waiting to go in after you." —**PAT LENTZ**

"Be aware of what characters look like on TV and in commercials and the movies—and with the 'powers that be' associate with a character. In other words, don't wear jeans if you have an audition for a woman who owns a jewelry store or, a panty hose commercial." —**JUDITH DRAKE**

"Most of us don't start out with life wisdom. I know I didn't! I wanted everyone to like me and I had to be perfect all the time. I would beat myself up or analyze myself to death, if I thought I made the slightest mistake, or could have been better on that line or my hair kinked up, or I wore the wrong outfit, and it went on and on and on. The practice of baring ourselves intimately to a room full of strangers time and time again ultimately disciplines us to find an inner strength and quieting of the mind. I do remember well the feelings of anxiety, upset stomach and nerves when I would enter an audition process and how much more intense those feelings would become as the process grew and it felt as if more was on the table to lose. That becomes exhausting! You find that often there is no rhyme or reason, your mind can come up with, that you did or did not land the job! If you try to make sense of this or obsess about it, you will drive yourself CRAZY! So, the good news is, you start to make the journey the destination and enjoy each moment fully." —**SHERRY HURSEY**

"Don't sit next to someone who is distracting or negative at an audition." —**ROBIN DEARDEN**

"Never second guess what the casting director or director is looking for. When you present yourself, don't be what you think they want you to be. Get comfortable in your own skin and be yourself." —**ANNE MARIE HOWARD**

"There's room for every type but, look your best until the breakdown says the character is slovenly. Having said that, try to figure out who you are and what you do well. This may come from doing lots of plays or scene study and discovering that there's a certain girl-next-door quality that comes through for you like no one else in your class. See if you can find scenes or write scenes to explore and exploit what you do well. This might give you confidence as well as narrow down how an agent or casting director sees you in the beginning. Being well defined at first could be a very good thing. There's something different, special and unique about you, but we may not see it clearly enough until you define it." —**ROBIN POLK**

"Oh, when I was younger, disappointments would break my heart. You give so much, and to be told 'No' could be devastating. But I soon learned that my job is to 'audition.' Not only book the job, but to audition. Once I learned that, I eased up on my nerves and also enjoyed the process more, which meant that I wasn't as needy, wasn't as nervous in the room. And, to also know that all directors, casting directors, producers, all those in the room making the decisions want you to be fantastic and to be 'the one' so they can stop looking. No matter what the vibe is when you walk in, all of them want to be wowed! And, why not let that be you. Keep yourself ready, keep yourself focused, keep yourself positive and always honest. I am not saying that you lie about your feelings, but don't let them keep you down. Sometimes it is very necessary to writhe in your pain, tears and moaning and all. I am saying 'Do NOT stay in it.' And, keep your eyes open for the gifts that come to you, because it is sometimes the little things that will change your life." —**IONA MORRIS**

CHAPTER 9

Unions Equal Power

You really can't work as an actor without belonging to a union, basically, SAG/AFTRA for TV and film and Actor's Equity for theatre. That fact can be a little hard to swallow for fledgling actors because it feels like a Catch-22; you have to be cast in a union role to qualify to join the union, but you ostensibly can't audition without a union card!

Obviously, opportunities arise for non-union actors to read for union-sanctioned projects, but it can be very frustrating at first. It's also a tough pill when you consider that once you are a dues-paying union member, there is absolutely no guarantee of work, and you more than likely will not be allowed to accept non-union work should it come your way.

Nevertheless, and in spite of the current political climate, we can't forget what life-saving changes the institution of unions into the American workplace created.

Today, we take for granted so many of their hard-won rights and protections and the empowerment they gave all working people by joining forces as one voice. It seems especially significant in the arts because, let's face it, most performers and crafts people would probably pay for the privilege of showing their art to an audience. Our desire is so strong we would forsake fair wages just for the pleasure of exercising our talent. So, it's all the more essential that we have the safety of numbers in a union to protect us not only from insufficient pay and demeaning working conditions by our employers, but from our own lack of respect for the value of what we do.

The workplace has changed significantly since we came up

through the ranks, especially with the advent of new media and technology. It is your job to be aware, prepared and to adjust to all the developments, challenges and changes coming down the road for actors. But the fundamental issues remain the same. While Internet content providers negotiate their pay structures actors must keep pace, and even try to anticipate the market demands. It seems the muscle of a unified voice would be even more valuable in this environment, so we advocate investing seriously in beefing up guild participation to insure that actors get their fair share of emerging entertainment platforms.

Without a strong union, you will have to accept much more personal responsibility for your work welfare and income security, and if our experience is any judge, most actors would rather focus their attention on performance than salary negotiation. Let Guilds and Agents do that work, but be sure they are representing you well.

A Love/Hate Relationship with the Unions

MOLLY: I thank the Gods for my guild pension and health benefits, but I have also had experiences where the union did not have my back.

DEBBIE: Me, too.

MOLLY: In one case, a group of soap opera performers, of whom I was one, received what seemed like unusually large residual checks. When actors called to verify the amounts, the union told us to go ahead and cash the checks only to find out the network had made a serious error and wanted all the money back a year later.

DEBBIE: OMG! I hate to say it but I have a love/hate relationship with my union because there have been a couple times when I was disappointed they didn't follow through on certain important issues. In one case, my safety had been at risk and another actor was injured on location and the union did nothing more than issue a letter of complaint. Maybe their hands were tied, or maybe it was up to me to push the union harder.

MOLLY: Yes.

DEBBIE: However, they made up for all of the disappointments and much, much more when fighting for commercial residuals a company was refusing to pay me. Even though the entire side of my face, or should we say profile, was in the commercial spot they said I wasn't recognizable as me. Therefore, I was just going to get the 'day wages' I had already been paid. NO residuals.

MOLLY: That can make you heart sick if it runs.

DEBBIE: YES, because I knew this commercial was going to really pay when it started airing, and it would air for a while. I had remembered that we improvised dialogue in the spot, so I called my union rep.

MOLLY: What did she do?

DEBBIE: She went to the company and requested a copy of the commercial. And there was my voice, and it was recognizable so once it aired I started to receive residuals, and by the time it was off the air I had made over $20,000 and was eligible for my health insurance.

MOLLY: Yoo-hoo! No one is looking out for you the way you look out for yourself.

DEBBIE: You have to be willing to fight when you feel a mistake has been made. But in this case the union made all the difference in the world and had my back. I am so grateful for my pension now and the access to health care my family and i have always had. And they are a valuable educational resource as well. They have great speakers in educational FREE seminars for actors on so many topics. It is just another way they support their members. The benefits far outweigh the disappointments.

Insight and Sage Advice from Well-Seasoned Actors

"Respect and get involved in your unions. Your unions are not your Mother or Father figures either! You are not entitled to a good career; you are responsible for making a good career which, with thought and industry, will provide health insurance and pensions." **—CLAUDETTE SUTHERLAND**

"Unions: A hot topic. Without our unions we as actors would be 'slave labor' literally. Before the formation of SAG/AFTRA actors could be required to work for hours on end, for very little money, without any safety regulations, breaks, forget meal penalties, overtime, trailers or residuals, I hear actors complain about their union and what it isn't doing for them. Instead, become involved, volunteer, connect and collaborate with your fellow union members to make SAG-AFTRA a better and stronger force for YOU." **—ROBERTA BASSIN**

"I am a 30-plus year union member. Work with your union. Find out what is available and how to make it work for you. They are there to help you. You will find a lot of producers who complain about how difficult it is to work with our unions. And, yes, there is that, but they are there to support their members. So, support them. Get familiar with your representatives, and always use them when you are in need." **—IONA MORRIS**

CHAPTER 10

Tooting Your Own Horn:
The Importance of Self-Promotion

When we were starting out, networking amounted to reading "Backstage;" dropping by your agent's office to keep your face fresh in their minds, getting in to the right party to schmooze the moguls and sending mass postcard mailings to announce a performance.

Like all fields, things are different in the entertainment industry today. We have a friend who is taking a social media class and tweeted a co-worker to congratulate him because she had heard he was directing a show. Boom, within no time he had a few lines written for her, and she was working the next week.

As with every other aspect of your career, the method you use to reach out and promote yourself is up to you.

It helps to keep in mind that "You the Actor" are a commodity that "You the Person" must advertise. Find ways to do that as effectively as you can. If clever repartee is not your strong suit, maybe Twitter isn't the smartest avenue. If you are awkward in large groups, don't rely solely on publicity events to keep you and your talent in the limelight.

Make peace with your strengths and weaknesses, and make realistic choices on how best to promote yourself. But do it!

It's all About Selling YOU

DEBBIE: I definitely was not good at promoting myself. If we had social media (i.e.: Twitter, Facebook, Linked In and so on) back in the good ole olden days, I think I would've been good at using that. There are even classes out there now for maximizing social media to help your career. But, as it is, I was very shy and felt dedicating myself to my craft was all I needed. I always wished I had done more socializing with other people in the business. You never know whom you'll meet, and maybe I could've found some relationships and made connections.

MOLLY: On the other hand, most of my breaks in show business came at the hands of strangers or possibly acquaintances. Not friends. Aside from the predatory and superficial aspects of mercenarily cultivating influential friends, the sheer truth of that fact will free up a lot of useless socializing to meet and befriend the "right" people.

DEBBIE: Yes. I do agree. However, remember that audition where I had to cry and I was terrified I would embarrass my husband? Well, I did get that audition by getting to know the producer/writers at the parties I went to because of my husband, who was on that show. I'm normally very shy at parties where I don't know people well, but I tried to make more of an effort in this case. And it paid off.

MOLLY: Again, it is an individual choice. I was so completely uncomfortable with the blurry lines between business and social, that I felt I wouldn't do myself any good showing up at events where I would most likely stand in the corner all night. So, I decided early on that if having an acting career required opportunistic socializing, I wouldn't pursue it. I couldn't abandon my peace of mind by doing something so unnatural for me.

DEBBIE: Again if you are not comfortable with it then no, it won't work. But I did know actresses who were good at the social aspect, and it helped them. And so looking back I needed to find a way to get comfortable with it. It is part of the business side of things and, as we say, you need to think of an acting career as a business. Networking is part of self-promotion. Hearing what others are doing or hearing about a part that might suit you as well gives you a reason to call your agent and touch base.

Unfortunately, I didn't see the beauty of that until much later in my career.

MOLLY: I especially regret falling for the advice everyone got as soon as they landed a series or big film: get a publicist. That really backfired for me because contrary to what everyone thinks about actors, I don't like to talk about myself or draw attention to me. And I'm a bad storyteller. Makes for a pretty dull interview, which is why "People" magazine didn't bother to run the piece they did on me. I was so embarrassed by that I decided I would let it all hang out for the next one, a "TV Guide" feature. The only thing more embarrassing than an unpublished interview is a published one that quotes you dishing dirt and making snotty remarks about co-stars. Did I really think William Shatner's pomposity or his girdle were entertaining fodder? It was horrible and made me look like a self-indulgent ingrate.

I definitely should have listened to my own heart and foregone the publicity route. Well, with one exception: I did get to win on *Password*!

DEBBIE: Even though you and I were a bad fit for the traditional publicity schmoozing route, I do think actresses can do themselves a world of good by promoting themselves properly. I guess they have to think of it as another valuable and vital tool in their acting business tool kit.

If they are not comfortable with it, like I wasn't, then they need to find a way to get comfortable with self-promotion on every level at every step in their career. Someone needed to tell me how utterly important it was. Perhaps I would have dedicated more of my time and energy towards improving those skills. I wish I had.

MOLLY: I've always thought seeing someone with real personality on a talk show can definitely increase their popularity. My step-daughter works for a big publicist, and I see how valuable it is for their clients to have her shepherding them through the red carpet hoopla and tracking all their media coverage. I think if I'd had someone that good to coach me on the interview process on a talk show it would've been a much more profitable experience.

DEBBIE: You bet. It pays to find the right people to surround yourself with, who can also boost your confidence level, and nowadays there are coaches and classes available for every aspect of your career. Because we must also be business people, we need to embrace and take responsibility for the promotion side of our career. You cannot expect the agent to do it all.

Insight and Sage Advice from Well-Seasoned Actors

"An actor friend of mine told me that he had trouble talking about his successes. He said it felt like he was bragging. No one is going to know what you've done unless you share it with them. When you have successes, share them with the world. Be bold. Brag a little!" —**ANNE MARIE HOWARD**

"You don't have to sell your soul to be successful…but you do have to know how to sell yourself." —**MARIANN AALDA**

"Would that I'd read a book like this when I was starting out. I know it would have provided much needed guidance. Here's what I've learned: you have to be your own agent and PR person—even if you have those types in your employ. Especially today when connecting with people—and I use the word connecting rather than networking—you cannot ignore the power of social media. I have heard more than once that potential show business employers care whether or not you have a network in place. It could even be the deciding factor in you or your competitor getting the job. Personally, I got a job recently simply because I reached out to a director I hadn't seen in thirty years on Facebook. A part suddenly came up, there was no time to 'cast,' so he literally went to Facebook to see who he 'knew.' I got an offer and became a true believer in the value of social media. Take my word for it. Twitter and Facebook allow you to connect with folks you probably couldn't get on the phone. If you build your online relationships carefully, you can open doors for yourself. I highly recommend people like Dallas Travers and Therese Cator who have developed marketing strategies specifically for the actor. Check them out. I've also (re)discovered that genuine enthusiasm is a highly desirable quality for a potential employer. When I run into, have lunch with, meet people who work on shows or have projects I'm interested in, I tell them, 'I'd love to work for you. I'd love to read for you anytime!' And I mean it. The worst that can happen is that they'll think, 'Oh, she's enthusiastic.' This is not a profession for the shy and retiring. It took me a long time to really learn that and embrace it. Any action you can take to empower yourself as an actor is worthwhile. It moves the molecules around and change happens!" —**PENNY PEYSER**

"This is very important. Keep your name out there. Your generation has Twitter, Facebook, Instagram, and so on. In my day, it was postcards and thank you notes. They all worked for the same purpose—to keep your name in people's faces. Remember, out of sight, out of mind. Be your own best PR person. Also, when you do get a PR person, don't rely upon them to do everything. Stay aware of what is going on. You are always your best promoter."
—**IONA MORRIS**

"If you are not well connected you have to shout very loud."
—**JUDITH DRAKE**

"It's understood that there will be peaks and valleys in every actor's career. But if you linger in the valley too long you run the risk of being forgotten about by the folks who have hired you before. Even worse—because gigs for casting directors, writers and producers can be just as transitory as those for actors—you may be a total unknown to the folks who might have replaced them!

The best way to get a job is when you've already got a job, or had a recent job. So an actor needs a resume that is current. This is hard to do when you haven't worked in a while. So the smart thing to do is to create your own project. Do you sing well enough to put together a cabaret act? Are you funny enough to do stand-up? Are you a good storyteller? Can you do magic?

Do you have friends you can collaborate with to form a sketch comedy troupe or produce a play to showcase yourselves? And once you've got your project up and running, don't forget to 'put it in a pretty package and tie a bow around it' by sending out email blasts, postcards, press releases and tweets no matter what the gig is. Unless you just got hired as the lead in a Steven Spielberg movie, it's not nearly as important for industry folks to know what you're working on as it is just to know that you're working." **—MARIANN AALDA**

CHAPTER 11

Separating the Person from the Performer

Before we were actors, we were people with all kinds of broad-ranging interests and experiences. When the show is over, we are still those people.

It's sometimes difficult to separate you—the person from you—the performer. The "winning isn't everything, it's the only thing" attitude that can serve us well as a motivational tool in this highly competitive field contributes to the difficulty in making that separation.

The industry rewards those who put on the blinders and focus with laser-intensity on "becoming the character," but it's important to stay connected to the person behind the role.

Walking into a producer's office with just yourself to sell is a scary and often lonely endeavor. In our experience, the fortitude to face those moments comes from balancing your focus by nurturing the other elements in your life. It's vital to make time and space for yourself—to reflect and absorb. Neglecting other interests, hobbies, people and issues comes at a price and is rarely worth it.

Be *More* Than an Actor

DEBBIE: My first acting teacher in college, Philip Taylor, once said, "Acting is a reflection of life. In order to reflect life you have to live it." Truer words were never said. I have reminded myself of those words through my life as an actress.

MOLLY: Keeping a healthy perspective is your life work whether you are an actor or a plumber. But again, because an actor's product is herself, and because the roles are sometimes few and far between, it's maybe even a little more challenging to remember that work is not the Be-All, End-All.

DEBBIE: We all think superstitiously from time to time as actor's, and I'm certainly guilty of this, that the minute we plan a vacation, the most perfect opportunity of a career will arise, and it will be missed. You just have to learn to yield to other important things in your life as a whole, or you will go nuts trying to reschedule, reshuffle and reorder your life around a single appointment or potential job.

MOLLY: Yes, your quality of life has to be equal to the whimsical promise of an audition. So live your life.

DEBBIE: When I was having labor pains and just about to go to the hospital to give birth to my first child, I actually got a call from my TV agent to see if I could go on an audition for a cable Disney series the next day. Can you believe it?

MOLLY: Yes and No. That's nuts!

DEBBIE: I tell you it killed me that I was not available. My brain raced to see how I could make it work. But I realized my insanity. I was, after all, about to give birth. Hello! Of course, once I had my baby girl in my arms a whole new perspective set in, and missing one audition was not worth any regret in comparison to this new blessing in my life.

MOLLY: Of course.

DEBBIE: I can't believe I gave it a second thought before the birth!

MOLLY: It comes with the territory. Actors tend to operate from that place of fear, but we have to strive for balance. And learn to trust that another audition or job will come down the pike.

DEBBIE: It's hard to do when you feel as I used to, that "Acting is who I am." Having my whole self-worth tied to whether I got that acting job was so unhealthy.

MOLLY: No one element should define who we are.

DEBBIE: I think what everyone needs to think about is, "What else?" Once in our group Actresses@Work, we had a psychologist as a guest speaker who said that we need to remember that we are a tapestry of talents and abilities; more than just one thing. It's important to recognize that in our selves. For one thing, the more of your interests and arts you nurture, the fuller your life experiences and the more you have to add to your acting toolbox. And for another, keeping all your avenues of creativity alive sustains you and feeds your self-esteem when you're faced with rejection for reasons like, "Your teeth are too big…"

MOLLY: Or, "Your boobs are too small."

DEBBIE: Or, "Your smile is too gummy."

MOLLY: Aaaah, not that! You know, something I wish I'd known before embarking on an acting career in Hollywood, is that there are innumerable other jobs in show business that tap into many of the same talents and sensibilities as acting. I often wondered if my intellect, as well as my self-respect, might have been better served by a career developing scripts for a studio or becoming part of the liaison team between TV shows and networks. Lots of creative qualities are required in jobs like those and a host of others that, until you spend time around the business, you wouldn't know existed.

DEBBIE: The advice I give to any young person wanting an acting career is, "Don't be *just* an actor." Be a writer. Be a producer. Investigate all those other creative outlets because you will find empowerment in creating your own work. You will have more options in your career, and you will walk into an audition with a bigger sense of pride in yourself because you are more than just an actor; you have a larger vision and acting is using only one of your many talents.

MOLLY: It's true that an actor going into an audition is not treated with the same respect as a producer going into a pitch session. We saw that so clearly going in for meetings with In The Trenches Productions.

DEBBIE: Yes! Psychologically, you tend to feel like you're always begging when you go in as an actor, where it's easier to feel you have something to give them as a producer. Even if they are thinking "Oh man, another meeting," they still have to be respectful because they don't know, you might have the next "American Idol" concept.

Actors need to adopt the producer mentality, that you have a gift to bring them. And if they say "No," it's to your project idea, not to you personally.

MOLLY: It's funny to think back when we were coming up and realize how much attitudes have changed. Then, it was considered a mistake to "split your focus" and attempt to develop other skills because you'd not be taken as seriously in your specific field.

DEBBIE: So true. I had a desire to produce early on, but actresses didn't have production companies in those days. Things are more open now, because actresses like Goldie Hawn took control and started their own production companies. The advances of technology have made tools available at a reasonable price to anyone so they can prep, edit, and do post-production for a movie in the comfort of their own home office. All these things open up so many more creative avenues. It is exciting and empowering, and it makes me think of something Erma Bombeck said, "When I stand before God at the end of my life, I would hope that I would have not a single bit of talent left, and I could say, 'I used every gift you gave me.'"

Insight and Sage Advice from Well-Seasoned Actors

"Honoring yourself and those you love will always help you make the right choice. Looking back, I remember booking a national American Express commercial that I was certain would pay my bills for some time and the very evening before the three day shoot, my husband suffered a stroke and I had to call paramedics to take him to the emergency room. There was no way I could work or give a decent performance with my husband needing me to be with him in intensive care. Of course, I turned down the job, but at 23, I was genuinely afraid I would never work again. I was truly touched and surprised when the casting office and the production office sent flowers and letters to the hospital. There will always be another opportunity." —SHERRY HURSEY

"Don't Limit Yourself. On Broadway you were a triple threat if you could sing, dance and act. Now, you need to learn everything about the business from acting, writing, directing, lighting, camera work, editing to line-producing, and more. You may end up liking one of these more or just having a great understanding of the business. Learn everything you can from everyone you can." —ROBIN POLK

"Being a successful and happy little actress ain't necessarily all about sobbing while clutching a golden statue—not that there's anything wrong with that. But there are other paths." —DORIS HESS

"I believe my career is simply what I do for a living. The truth is, the other areas of my life, my family, my faith, my charity work, and so on, are more interesting and contribute more to my well-being, than does my career. Balance isn't simply something to desire, it is critical to sanity and survival. I am a huge advocate of volunteering. No matter how poorly your career may be going, if you are engaged in helping others you maintain your self- worth and confidence every time you look into the face of the person who are helping." —**MARIANNE MUELLERLEILE**

"A wise old actor once told me that all actors need to learn to 'go fishing' in-between their acting jobs. Later in life, I understood the meaning of this statement. Enjoy all aspects of your life. Learn new things, take time to explore, be curious and adventurous. It will all be helpful for your acting. Real life makes you who you are." —**ANNE MARIE HOWARD**

"Somehow I knew from a very early age that creating a character came from understanding the LIFE of that person. As I matured and came to realize that if I didn't live a full and balanced life outside of just 'being an Actor,' I would have little to bring to my acting except my 'idea' of what the character felt. Also, the business, being as capricious as it is, is not the basis one wants to base one's happiness on. I've come to know that it is so much wiser and emotionally healthy to experience a whole life filled with love, friends, family and other activities. If I can help to impart this to a new generation of actresses, I will feel very gratified." —**JANICE KENT**

"There are SO many areas of interest that never crossed my mind. I was so bent on becoming a great actress, that things like tele-journalism, or broadcast news, or political office –all of which still puts one in the 'eye of the camera,' so to speak, you are still 'on'—were never considered, or even thought of. I was doggedly single-minded in my pursuit of being an actress. Maybe that is what it takes to succeed, or at the very least, to know, completely, that you gave it your all your very best shot." —**DEBORAH MAY**

"A well-informed actress is an interesting actress. When you are playing a part, you pull in everything you know. Now, in regards to avenues outside this business: 1) There is public speaking, inspiring others—and who better to share stories and to present themselves with joy, energy and remain engaging, but an actress? 2) Hobbies—always great to have a full life because that keeps you sharp, keeps you interested and interesting. In my youth, I put all my time into my work, and I feel I missed a lot of opportunities to experience more of this world. I have changed that and have found myself much happier. Acting is what I do, but it is not who I am. 3) Write, direct, paint, etc. I also started directing about 15 years ago—which was another thing that came to me when the auditions weren't coming in as frequently.

"I have directed one-person shows, large musicals and dramatic plays. I find this makes me so much happier. Just relying on acting is quite frustrating. Find other creative ways to express yourself. The triple threat used to be that of 'dancer, singer, actress.' It is now 'actress, writer, director' and you can add producer to that and you have a quadruple threat ready to make magic. Exercise your creative muscles and see where they take you. Do NOT sit and wait for the phone to ring, for someone else to allow you to be creative. If you aren't auditioning or booking, write your own material and put it on the web, put it on the stage, film, television. What else can you do that keeps your imagination firing on all cylinders? Don't allow yourself to get stuck in one thing no matter what that is. You are more than one talent. Are you an actress, painter, singer? Are you an actress, writer, chef?

"Widen your horizons. You will be more open, more available, more interesting, and happier in mind, heart and spirit. I will continue to say, be the best YOU that you can be and support her because she is your best friend. What makes you stand out from all the rest? Being the best YOU, you can be. You aren't competing with anyone, but yourself. Support you. Give you all you need, to be the best more interesting, most engaging, most available YOU that you can be. I have great friends. I traveled, I fell in love with cooking and learned how to whip up some great meals, I kept my mind open to other adventures in my life. I didn't really learn till later in life, (around 40) that having a balanced life, yoga, meditating, journaling, traveling, educating myself about things that didn't have to do with the entertainment business, would keep me sharp and more available to my craft. I thought it would take me away, so I kept my mind on auditions and working.

"Life is about living. Life is not about working, it is not about being an actress. It's about experiencing yourself in this world and bringing all you are to your craft when you do work. This makes you much more interesting." —IONA MORRIS

CHAPTER 12

Surviving the Insecurities of Show Business

Even if you are fortunate enough to earn as much money as you need without working a second job, there is a psychological price for the free-lance nature of acting.

Insecurity and disappointment are part and parcel of a career in the arts and takes a toll on you. How do you keep your self-esteem intact? How do you keep from taking the criticism and rejection to heart without questioning your talent? By recognizing your performance is not all of you.

This work requires a great deal of inner strength and resourcefulness. Choosing this career involves learning how to stay centered through insight and reflection in order to manage the obstacles you will face—with poise. It's an ongoing struggle made even more difficult by the fact that the product you are peddling is you. A sense of humor and an ability to laugh are remarkable coping tools, by the way.

Time and experience will be your best teachers.

How *Not* To Take It Personally

DEBBIE: You go on audition after audition and most of the time you are rejected. Many times it is something about you physically or a personality thing that they cite for you not getting the role.

MOLLY: Everything is so subjective when it comes to art. So you need to know it is not a judgment of you as a human being.

DEBBIE: One of the hardest lessons is learning how to keep from taking any of it personally. That is very tricky.

MOLLY: A heartbreaker for me was the Lindsay Wagner pilot *Jessie*. I was so pleased to have gotten the more character-like side kick role and thrilled to get the call from the producers saying the show had been picked up, but my practical side prompted me to follow my congratulations to them with a concern. "You know, I kind of wonder where my character really fits in as the story develops. I mean, I would completely understand if she didn't make it to the series."

DEBBIE: How good of you!

MOLLY: And the producers said, "We wouldn't do it without you," to which I said, "Okay because I'm planning on buying a new car. Do you think I should go ahead?" And they said yes.

DEBBIE: Awwww.

MOLLY: Two weeks later, guess who was not on the show anymore? But that is the thing, you just can't take something like that personally. There is nothing I could have done about that. They had written that character into a corner. It wasn't my fault. I suppose if I had been some breakout Swoozie Kurtz or somebody I could have made such a big impression on the part that they couldn't do without me, but it was highly unlikely.

The point is, you're at the whim of so many other forces, and your control over it is miniscule.

DEBBIE: I remember a time when I was up for a bug spray commercial and eventually it was down to the wire. They finally decided against me because they thought I was too young to have roaches—like roaches have some kind of target age group! It was so off the wall, I never forgot. Of course, it's nice to hear you are too young for something!

MOLLY: But still, what do you do with that? You can't perform your way out of it. There's just nothing in your control there.

DEBBIE: You have to account for their lack of imagination is all. You gotta be able to laugh, and you especially need to be able to laugh at yourself. The constant rejection can rip at your soul. Even just the obsessing over whether or not you got the job, all the self-doubt takes a real toll. So, after every bad experience or important job loss, I highly recommend sitting with those feelings and crying for a day.

MOLLY: Yes, mourn. And then pop back up and find a way to move on to the next rejection.

DEBBIE: You mean, opportunity!

MOLLY: Of course.

DEBBIE: I was once told early in my career that I had gotten a regular role in a series. I went out and celebrated with friends and was on top of the moon. Then, I got the call that my agent had made a mistake, and I was just going in for another call-back. I'll never forget that cruel twist of fate. Disappointments come in all shapes and sizes, and I think each actor has to find her own way of handling them.

My advice is to keep your loved ones close, both friends and family. Make frequent calls, do lunch, and stay really connected to the people you love and who love and support you—no matter what.

MOLLY: Having those solid relationships is key to my peace of mind at the end of the day. I think that's true no matter what business you are in.

DEBBIE: And some of those relationships might be with other actors who are your competition.

MOLLY: Well, maybe that's why I had no actress friends!

DEBBIE: Oh dear, all of mine were actresses.

MOLLY: How did you manage to stay friends without being jealous when they were working or apologetic to them when you were doing well?

DEBBIE: Well I was jealous, and it made me feel like a lousy person.

MOLLY: At some point I realized that as long as I was getting a good enough percentage of the roles I was auditioning for, I could accept not getting them all. So why begrudge anyone else the part?

DEBBIE: First you love the friend no matter what and keep your jealousy to yourself. But as I matured and time went on, I adopted the perspective that I wanted them to work. I wasn't wishing them ill. I just wanted to work, too. And as long as I got my fair share, I talked myself in to not being stingy—unless they weren't friends, and I didn't like them or respect their talent. That was really difficult if I didn't think they deserved it.

MOLLY: So ultimately the actresses you were friends with, you also respected.

DEBBIE: Yes, and I needed their friendship. My gut feeling was when I was up and they were down, they would go through the same feelings, but the friendship always came first, and so we supported each other however we could.

MOLLY: You have to find the places and people that make you feel good about yourself when you feel like a failure. And you need them as a counterweight to the often negative general attitude that actors face. I mean, as much as society–at–large seems to shower adoration on performers, people actually in the business frequently resent and dismiss us. We get pinned with that flighty, neurotic, self-obsessed stereotype, which I found surprising—and yet another obstacle to overcome. It's kind of a love-hate deal because they need us, but don't necessarily like or respect us.

DEBBIE: My strong family ties, my marriage and my friendships are what center me—and what gives me strength and courage. They love me for who I am as a person, not who I am as an actress or what my last job was. It was key to surviving the rejection in my acting career.

MOLLY: And let's not forget the value of a good shrink.

DEBBIE: Is there such a thing as an actress who hasn't been to therapy?

MOLLY: Not likely.

DEBBIE: Well, I didn't go till my 30's, and not for long. So if your friends aren't available and you can't afford therapy, whatever the hurdles, you have to find tools to deal with the disappointments even if it is a crying jag for a day or two, or just working in the garden. And you need to create a support system. You just have to find a way to hang on to your belief in your talent and abilities. You know, you come with a dream, thinking if you have special talent and passion, doors will open, but it's not always the case.

My daughter once asked when watching the Academy Awards why I wasn't up there accepting a Best Actress Award. It hit me hard. I never questioned my talent.

My belief never wavered. As hard as I have worked and as much as I deserved those kinds of roles and that kind of recognition, it just hadn't and didn't happen. And ultimately, getting an Academy Award is as much about luck and timing as anything else, so I realized it was time to stop blaming myself or hitting my head against a wall.

Oscar or not, top of the heap or not, I was blessed with a talent that allowed me to make a living doing what I loved, and no one can ever take that away.

MOLLY: Not so for me, though ultimately, I arrived at the same moment of acceptance. I may have dreamt of big success, but it wasn't connected to a belief that I had that caliber of talent. For a long time, that recognition kind of tormented me, but eventually I made peace with what my limitations were and put my focus on the strengths I did have. Eventually I stopped beating myself up for not getting work that just wasn't in my wheelhouse.

DEBBIE: Eleanor Roosevelt once said, "Nobody can make you feel inferior without your consent." So you have the power to choose how you react to a situation.

MOLLY: Yeah, I think it's a huge life lesson to understand that no matter how your life goes, in the end, all you really have is the grace with which you handled it.

DEBBIE: Yes! That's it. That's what you hold onto and take stock in: how you managed your life, the bad and good situations. That is what will give you comfort in the long run.

MOLLY: The hurt of any immediate experience will diminish over time, but you hang on to "I behaved in a way I'm proud of."

DEBBIE: And I didn't let it get me down, and it didn't make me quit!

Insight and Sage Advice from Well-Seasoned Actors

"Every Saturday night for thirteen years I'd get together with my pals and do an Improv show—primarily because it reminded ourselves that we did have talent, and that our work was deserving of respect. And, it was such fun and so very releasing. We performed because we cared about and supported each other in every way and that gave each of us the courage and determination to get out there and go to the next audition with strength, self-respect and even joy." **—DORIS HESS**

"You cannot take it personally. Yikes! I had a producer call me and tell me that he loved the commercial I shot with his ad agen-

cy a week prior and that I wasn't going to get the job I just auditioned for because his small agency only had three clients, and when they sent out their reel it would look like they were only casting from a very small pool of talent if they used me again."
—ROBIN POLK

"Reporters who have never met you will write things about you that just aren't true. It happened to me while I was on *Another World*. It was upsetting at the time, but now I've learned that it's good to be talked about and that people will say whatever they want to say anyway. Don't dwell on it. Let it go. Pay attention to the good things that are being said about you. There will be far more positive comments. Enjoy them!" **—ANN MARIE HOWARD**

"When the phone is not ringing, when you are auditioning, but can't seem to book anything, you need a full life with other interests to support your being, to support your heart, to support your dreams. To keep you positive and present and ready for the next job that will come your way. There is always another one. Being pretty, having a killer body goes away with time. Sure, as we age, we keep our bodies in shape, but soon, a pretty, younger version will show up and she'll be the hot topic. This can't be the only thing in your life. Find other interests—like spending time finding and working your hobbies; making time for your family; teaching, or volunteering. Give yourself a reason to live that doesn't have to do with acting. This is an unpredictable business. If you let it run your life, you will be at its mercy. Don't do that to beautiful you. Be more than just an actress, be a full human being, whose love is acting, but who is so much more. That will keep you in a more positive light and give you the ability to weather all the storms. Cause, baby, as an actress, you will face some storms. Remember, it's not when or if you fall or will be knocked down; it's how you get up. And, you want to keep yourself fortified so that you can 'GET UP!'" **—IONA MORRIS**

"I have always loved the phrase, 'Fail your way to the top.' You can't fail if you don't take chances, and you can't move ahead if you don't fail along the way. Failing is how we learn. If you keep this in mind as you are auditioning, you will learn not to take anything personal." —SUE MULLEN

"I knew my thing was comedy so I never pushed for dramatic auditions. However, I also knew that drama is easier. Whenever I have done something dramatic in an acting class it really impresses people since they don't expect it from me. I did have one audition for a great guest spot on a popular hour-long drama. I found out from the casting director that when I left the room all the producers were blown away by my performance. They said that it was obviously the best read. But they decided that they couldn't give me the part since they feared that 'the girl who does sketches with Johnny Carson' would be too distracting for the audience's belief system. So sometimes you have to remember that you might not get a part simply because you are too associated with something else. And another time I received a phone call from a producer who told me that she wanted me to know that I had given a great audition. The network was going to make an offer to a certain star. But if the star turned down the offer, I was the producer's first choice. I was so grateful for that call. As actors we assume the worst, that we did something wrong when often it's just a matter of the network having to go for the biggest names they can." —TERESA GANZEL

"Where thoughts go, energy flows. Make sure your thoughts are positive. Surround yourself with supportive, loving friends. If they're not behind you 100 percent, they're not good for you. Envision yourself succeeding. See it, feel it, breathe it in and out. You are everything you imagine yourself to be. Imagine yourself wildly successful." —ANNE MARIE HOWARD

"When you come to Hollywood, or, no doubt, NY, you've got to create your safe places. It could be joining a church, taking a yoga or dance class, playing on a softball team, or getting into a good acting class. Surround yourself with healthy, supportive people. This is key because some people can suck the life right out of you if you let them." —**MAGGIE EGAN-CUMMINGS**

"The one thing to always remember is to be your own best friend. Keep yourself engaged in life, not in acting, singing, and writing. Find a spiritual connection to yourself and to the powers who give you breath of life, keep your skills sharp, have fun, be joyful, know that all your defeats bring you closer to your wins, they make you stronger, there are no accidents, there are no mistakes, they are only lessons to fortify you and get you ready for the good that is coming." —**IONA MORRIS**

"Don't take it personally. Your competitor may well have gotten the job simply because she had brown eyes and you didn't." —**JUDITH DRAKE**

"I believe it is important to have a nice, clean place to live with lots of light, a place to work, healthy food, exercise, healthy friends and a strong desire to give." —**BETH GRANT**

"The joy and the jobs really flow when you stop identifying yourself with your talents and just let yourself be a channel for them. You are BIGGER than your face, your voice, your skills, and your talent! You must find that center within yourself and love it! You are only defeated when you let yourself feel defeat! The you that is YOU cannot be defeated! What you truly believe about yourself, others will believe also!" —**SHERRY HURSEY**

"In my later years, as I did when I was younger, I wanted a committed relationship. I found that I wanted someone who loved me for me. Someone I could come home to. I was finding my love in my work and that is so subjective and also not consistent. I learned that I was so much into myself and my work that I wasn't always making myself available, even to men I liked. So, I turned my plate into a platter and gave time to a wonderful man who I have now been with for 11 years and, going strong. I have also been spending more time with friends, traveling, going to museums, taking classes, volunteering more, I don't think about whether the phone is ringing or not so much. I am more joyful and more available and ready for auditions when they come my way." —IONA MORRIS

CHAPTER 13

Actors Are Storytellers

The abundance of tabloid magazines and paparazzi and the out-sized millions of dollars that actors can command as film and TV stars can obscure the importance actors have in the world. The superficial perks of celebrity can crowd out our seeing the commitment and sacrifices actors make in order to practice their craft—which is, to bring to life the stories that bind us together as a people.

Sharing stories is a basic human need. For thousands of years, great stories have had tremendous impact on mankind. They connect us to our history, spark our imaginations, provoke deep emotion, awaken our spirits, compel us to explore, dream, and act with greater courage and compassion.

Actors are our storytellers—the vehicles that deliver the messages and emotions so essential to the fabric of humankind. As if by magic, they transform our stories into living, breathing entities and in doing so reach, into and elevate our collective souls.

Acting is a Noble and Honorable Profession—and Fun, Too!

MOLLY: I had never thought of it that way. I always thought it was a pretty selfish and light-weight profession. But, recognizing how deep an impact so many performances have had on my life, I've gradually allowed myself to extend to my own work some of the same respect I give other actors.

DEBBIE: I didn't really think about the importance of the acting profession either. I was just blinded by love. But now looking back I realize the significance. Even when I watch a lousy movie, TV show or piece of theatre where the lofty or intended vision has completely failed, if there is even just one perfect inspired magical moment by a wonderful actor that transcends the piece it is well worth sitting through.

MOLLY: What we *have* known all along was that the many, many joys of being a working actor out-weigh the downside by a considerable margin. From the "You got the part!" phone call to the thrill of working opposite people whose work you've admired (and then realizing that in working with them, you can hold your own), to the simple pleasure of giving your friends and family access to the "glamorous" world of show business—there are so many rewards.

DEBBIE: There was nothing better than the moment I got that first job. My heart felt like it would burst. But even better, was getting to work in front of a camera for the first time and being on an actual television set shooting on the same lot as "Towering Inferno." Since then there have been many moments where I relished and cherished that call of victory where I was told I got the job and every single moment I was working. It was like being in the best playground with all these great playmates.

MOLLY: I often think how I can count on one hand the performances in my career that truly soared. But that handful flew straight into the heavens for me and made the entire rest of my working life worthwhile. It's that powerful when it hits.

DEBBIE: Those moments, the joy I felt when playing a character honestly and truthfully that touched an audience, will live in my heart forever.

When the planets align, when you hit those artistic moments in your craft that are sheer perfection, when you achieve what you rehearsed and thought about and serve the material to the best of your ability and hear the positive response from those watching you perform at the top of your game there is no greater joy even if it is in a piece of crap.

As much as being an actor can tear at your soul, your confidence and self-esteem, when you overcome your fears and meet the challenge you get all that back and so much more. And it doesn't matter where this happens. Whether you are on the set of a major motion picture in a lead role or co-starring on a TV show, in an audition with a room of insensitive or distracted suits, on stage with a packed audience or in a class with a few respected contemporaries, making your performance as an actress sing is better than dark chocolate, vintage wine, pizza and sex put together! No matter what I do, what project or job I take in the future or how rewarding another path or career is, nothing will ever be on the level of the joy I found as an actress.

Insight and Sage Advice from Well-Seasoned Actors

"Acting is a noble profession despite the celebrity gossip mill. Ever since tribes gathered around campfires to act out the adventures of the day's hunt, humans have been captivated by the cathartic pleasures of story-telling and make believe. At these early campfires I'm sure there was one person who could tell the story better than anyone in the tribe. 'Egor, shut up and let Bruno tell the story.' Anyone who is drawn to the profession actually can't help themselves; it seems written in their DNA to act. And all actors are undoubtedly descendants of those first storytellers. Civilization needs actors. Actors allow the tribe to learn life lessons in an entertaining form, to laugh to relieve the tension of everyday life, to cry, to dream, to fantasize, to feel that they are part of the tribe. From storytellers in the caves, to Ancient Greek and Roman Theatre, to Shakespeare, to Molière, to Oscar Wilde to Broadway—every era has had theatre as an integral part of society. While actors have been much maligned, the profession in its purest form does a huge service for the community."
—JAN BINA

"Now I kind of wish I weren't retired. Although I cannot deny that there were times when it would have been more pleasant to just slam my hand repeatedly in a car door, my life as an actress was mostly a source of satisfaction and delightful surprises."
—DORIS HESS

"If you don't become a celebrity actor, you can still be an actor. And even good utility players can earn a living and receive a pension, plus we get to go out with friends and family without having people snapping our pictures that end up in tabloids showing us with salad dressing dripping down our chin." **—MAGGIE EGAN-CUMMINGS**

"Like music and art, acting moves people: it makes them feel, cry, laugh. To be in a darkened theatre and hear people cry because your character is in pain is very powerful. I think acting creates a catharsis for people, for the actor and the audience. When you laugh so hard you're crying watching that actor, it stays with you and it will be repeated at dinner tables and parties. 'Oh you've got to see this play, I laughed so hard because this guy is so funny.' I think there's a little bit of immortality about acting knowing that for a brief moment you made somebody feel, maybe a moment they'll never forget." **—ROBIN DEARDEN**

"Acting is a service position. We are there to serve the play, the director's vision, to reveal our souls for the higher good."
—BETH GRANT

"A friend took me to see the play *Awake and Sing* on Sunday because her husband was out of town. It was great to see a good live performance and to hear someone who's not in the business talk about how important it is to support the arts. Rosalie told me that she feels people need actors to make them laugh and cry and experience other worlds and relationships to be more emotionally connected, especially in this age of technology. It was nice to hear someone appreciate the fact that there are people passionate about acting." **—ROBIN POLK**

"You never know how what you do will positively affect someone. I loved doing game shows as a 'celebrity' contestant, especially, *The $25,000 Pyramid*. I cannot tell you how many times at the supermarket or mall, and people would come up to me and thank me for helping them with the English language. So many people from other countries would use that show to help them learn language skills. And what better way to learn communication than through a word association game!" —**TERESA GANZEL**

"In my thirties, when I was doing a lot of commercials and guest roles in Hollywood, I was able to be a really hands-on mother to my two daughters because I could (almost always) schedule my life around my girls. Show business has always been a fortunate life for me—not only as an artist able to express, but as a person, meeting wonderful and forever friends throughout my life in the entertainment industry. PS: my daughters turned out to be fabulous young women!" —**MURPHY CROSS**

"What a gift of knowledge and experience acting has given me; an in-depth study of human nature, behavior and communication, wrapped up and delivered in a package of joyful self-discovery. The journey of acting has taught me to stay connected with the divine presence in me and to embrace myself wholly/holy! I AM so grateful for all of it! It has been and continues to be a brilliant ride, and I wouldn't trade it for the world!" —**SHERRY HURSEY**

"Working with STARS! I was star-struck as a kid and watched TV non-stop. Every week I read the 'TV Guide' cover to cover. I wanted to be an actress; I wanted to be Marlo Thomas in the sitcom, *That Girl*. When I started working as an actress I was blown away by the stars I got to work with. I got to be a series regular on a sitcom pilot with Ted Bessell. He was Marlo's boyfriend, and I was working right alongside him! The list of huge stars that I worked with that I had been idolizing since kindergarten still amazes me. Stars that I was doing impressions of during school recess I found myself laughing with. And almost always, the bigger the star, the better the experience. I have found that it was always the biggest stars that were the kindest to me. And the bigger stars that I got to work with always made me a better actor. And as far as rewards go…I may have had lots of disappointments as an actor. But the positive has far outweighed the negative. And I still believe more positive acting experiences are on the way for me." —**TERESA GANZEL**

"Acting gave me a sense of belonging. The most memorable moment: A play in college I'm sitting on the floor behind the scene going on, simply listening but my face was showing my thoughts, because suddenly the audience erupted with a huge laugh that had nothing to do with the actors in the scene, but with my reaction it was at that moment that I said to myself this is where I belong I have a presence people watch me. And my three-year mental tug-of-war over teaching or acting ended." —**JUDITH DRAKE**

"If you are fated to pursue this career, your joys can be many, if you don't get too hung up on stardom. If you view each audition as the reward in and of itself; if you stay humble, keep growing and stay courageous and not be afraid to take risks, you may experience wonderful and thrilling moments of fantasy that take you to glorious emotional heights. Is it easy to get to those moments of pure joy where you are totally in your fantasy world? No, of course not, but the desire for that rush is very strong and very addicting. I, for one, am glad I have been blessed to have a life as an actor." —**JAN BINA**

"I feel most alive when I am involved in putting together a cabaret act, or rehearsing a play, or when the director calls 'action' on a set. I love hearing the words, 'You got the job,' when my agent calls. I love directing a group of teenagers for a school production. I love the creativity and collaboration. My love for acting is greater than my greatest disappointment in acting. That's why I still love every opportunity I get to act. It truly has been a driving force in my life. I had to pursue this career, just like those dancers in *A Chorus Line* have to dance. That may be the common denominator here: desire and tenacity. Clearly, we all reach different levels of celebrity or fame which is what 'we,' society, tend to measure success by, but it isn't the only measure of success. I encourage the artists out there with a strong, unyielding whisper in their heart that tells them they need to perform to do just that. Write down some actions you can take today. Be the bravest person you know today, and take those small steps and just build on that. And remember, faith is coming to the edge of everything you know and jumping off that cliff knowing that either of two things will happen. Either you will learn to fly or you will find a safe place to land." —MAGGIE EGAN-CUMMINGS

"I love acting because it allows audiences to leave their day behind and join me in the character, in the moments I have created. It is a craft that can inspire, uplift and make the world a happier place. It is us, the artists, who change the world who put up a mirror for the world to see itself without reservation. It is the artist who can present a new and more expansive idea about the world. It is the artist who makes the world laugh, cry when shown things that need immediate changing, to widen our ideas of what our world is about. Your story of how you got here inspires the young girl or boy who wants to also be creative and use their voice to shine a light on the world condition. We are the ambassadors to the truth, to the mysteries of the soul, to stories in history that have been forgotten, cultures that have never been seen before or to shine a light on things that need healing. We are missionaries, healers, the buffoons who make the world laugh when they feel like crying. I love acting. I can play characters I don't get to live in my life. It is an exhilarating, bumpy ride and I love it! This is a very special club you belong to or are going to belong to. I wish you well, and I wish you joy and I wish you success! Go get 'em, girl! They are waiting for you!" —IONA MORRIS

CHAPTER 14

Be Ready for Your "Break-Out" Moment

Should you choose to pursue an acting career, we hope you experience the special joy and deep passion for the craft that we have. This profession will compel and propel you to meet, face and deal with some very real challenges. We hope this book of "insight and sage advice" from those who have been there gives you the guidance and perspective you need and will, lead you to your very special "break-out" moment.

We still want you to dream big and go for that Academy, Emmy, Tony, Cesar or Olivier Award and the "big bucks". Just remember that longevity is the Holy Grail of every acting career. Degrees of success will vary throughout, but the ability to keep working at the job you love is the real goal we wish for all of you. We believe the advice we've imparted is all geared toward that objective. If you take responsibility for your artistic, personal, and business health, you will be able to stay in the game as long as you desire.

We want to leave you with the single-most important message we have: Your way is the right way. The more of yourself you bring to the work, the better the work. The more meticulous you are about conducting the business of acting and controlling your finances, staying tuned-up and on top of the many self-promotion tools available, the longer run you will have.

We believe you are a success if you feel you gave the best performance you had in you, and you accepted the results with grace.

So, stay the course and above all, honor your journey in your own way.

About the Authors

MOLLY CHEEK

A familiar face to motion picture, television and theater audiences, Molly Cheek continues to amass credits in all three media fields. Molly is perhaps best known for her work as Jim's Mom in the "American Pie" films. Her additional feature film credits include "Smoke Signals;" "Spider-Man II;" "Drag Me to Hell;" and, "A Lot Like Love."

Molly's resume boasts of numerous TV pilots, guest appearances, short-lived series and a single Broadway performance in the staged reading of Alan Zweibel's tribute to Gilda Radner, "Bunny, Bunny." That aside, her most notable credits include four seasons of co-starring on Showtime's ground-breaking series, "It's Garry Shandling's Show" and three seasons as Mrs. Henderson opposite Bruce Davison in the syndicated TV series, "Harry and the Hendersons."

Cheek has appeared in countless television series as a regular on "The Yeagers," "Chicago Story" and "Go Fish" and guest-starred on a number of shows including "New Girl", "Without A Trace," "Cold Case," "Ellen," "St. Elsewhere," "Family Ties" and numerous others. She has appeared as a series regular on the pilots "1973," "Home of the Brave," "Beanpole," "No Place Like Home" and, "Jessie."

Molly's stage credits include "Mirage A' Trois" at the Santa Monica Playhouse, "Monkey Grass" at the Victory Theatre, "The Max Factor" at the Drury Lane," "Sunrise Over Manhattan" at Westbeth Music Center, and; "Encounter with Murder."

In between all Molly's film and TV work, she co-wrote/produced and directed the short film "Sick Chick" based on Cathy Cahn's one-woman show chronicling the absurdities of dealing with the medical world post-transplant.

DEBBIE ZIPP

Debbie Zipp is best known for her recurring lead role as Donna on the "Murder She Wrote" CBS series starring Angela Lansbury, as well as her principal roles in over 300 national television commercials. A few of her leading stage roles in Los Angeles include Judy in the Victory Theatre production of "Sirens of Seduction," Gracie in "Let's Get The Whole Thing Gershwin" at the Westwood Playhouse, and Debbie in "The Good One" at the Pan Andreas. She's had lead series regular roles in the television series pilots "The Cheerleaders" with Richard Crenna directing and "There's Always Room" also starring Maureen Stapleton. She also starred with Darren McGavin in the TV series "Small and Frye" for Disney.

Just a few of the TV series she guest-starred on include "Gilmore Girls;" "Malcom In The Middle;" "Magnum PI;" "Paper Chase;" "LA Law;" "New Love American Style;" and, "One Day At a Time." She appeared in such films as "Like Father Like Son" and "Double Exposure." Her short film credits are "Living Large With Less;" "Believe It Baby;" "Girltox;" and, "Welcome To My Garden."

Debbie was President of the non-profit activist organization *Actresses@Work* which helped lead the fight against ageism for women in the entertainment industry. She was Executive Producer of the documentary short "Invisible Women," three PSA'S on ageism and the stage production of "Magpie's Tea Room." She also produced the documentary short "The Forgotten Grave."

Debbie co-founded the production company IN THE TRENCHES PRODUCTIONS whose films must star a woman over 40. Debbie spearheaded the creation and development of the IN THE TRENCHES PRODUCTIONS Website, the first entertainment website for women over 40, where she produced many short films. Debbie also co-produces, co-writes and co-hosts the TOMATOES IN THE TRENCHES Blog Talk Radio Show, which is a lively gabfest for smart women over 40. Presently Debbie is the West Coast Editor for popular website THE THREE TOMATOES.

For workshops, seminars, webinars, or more information, visit the authors' webpage at:

www.AspiringActorsHandbooks.com

Appendix A

THE ASPIRING ACTOR'S WORKBOOK:

Questions We Wish We'd Asked Ourselves That Can Help You Think About The Choices Ahead of You

With the "insider" glimpse our book provides, you should be ahead of the game in terms of what your decision to choose an acting career entails. The pursuit of your dream should take into account a certain amount of self-examination, and we feel strongly that the more specific the questions you ask yourself and the more precise your answers—the better prepared you will be to move forward. To that end, we have developed a list of pertinent questions to guide you in the many choices ahead of you. We encourage you to read each question carefully, ponder them for a bit, and then write out your responses. The very act of writing down your plans and goals can more readily help you bring your dreams to fruition.

Consider starting a journal to record your answers and chart your growth. An important decision and plan like this is a process of self-discovery and growth that unfolds and develops at different speeds for each person, depending upon his or her individual circumstances. You may not be ready to answer some of these questions yet. So research, study and continue to reflect on the questions we've presented. Your answers may change during this process, and that is okay, because as an actor you will need to be flexible and open to change.

You have begun the journey by reading our book; now you're already on your way!

1. After reading this book, what advice or message most resonated with you? Give an example of how it affected you.

_____

_____

2. Which actors in the book strike a chord with you? What about them makes you relate to each?

_____

_____

3. Roberta Bassin spoke of "Naively thinking she had a choice" to be an actor. In what way do you have a choice in your decision?

_____

_____

4. List the top 5 reasons you want to be an actor, and then, using a 1 to 5 scale, with 1 being your number one reason and so on, rank them in order of their importance to you.

_____

_____

_____

_____

_____

5. Debbie Zipp made the point that it is important to consider "what else" you are besides an actor. List three other interests, talents and skills you possess. If you were to pursue one of those interests as a career, which one would that be?

_____

_____

_____

6. List 3 reasons you would pursue this career and rank these reasons in order of importance.

_____

_____

_____

7. In looking at your desire to pursue an acting career, and then in looking at your "secondary choice" for a career, which of these is the most desirable, and why is it the most compelling job choice for you?

_____

_____

8. In the book, various SAG/AFTRA employment statistics were cited. Describe how you feel about them in relation to your ideas of achieving "stardom."

_____

_____

9. List 6 actors you admire most in the worlds of film, television and stage today. Describe why you admire each one.

Who:_____

Why:_____

Who:_____

Why:_____

Who:_____

Why:_____

Who:_____

Why: _____

Who: _____
Why: _____

Who: _____
Why: _____

10. If being a full-time actor isn't something you can pursue right now, what other ways can you get your desire to entertain met? For example, would acting as an avocation—such as in community theatre—be satisfying to you? Why or why not?

_____

_____

11. What is the difference between acting and performing? Describe which one is of most interest to you. Which one best suits you?

_____

_____

12. How do you know you have sufficient confidence in yourself and your abilities, and the courage to approach a professional acting career?

_____

_____

13. Is your belief in your talent based most on response to your performances, or on your own gut feeling? How do you know? Give an example.

_____

_____

14. The authors spoke about the importance of being "temperamentally suited" to the free-lance lifestyle acting imposes. List 3 personality traits that support your belief that you could handle the instability and uncertainty of that world.

_____

_____

15. Self-motivation is a vital asset in an acting career. Are you self-motivated? Give an example that best shows you are.

_____

_____

16. Do you feel you can handle rejection without getting discouraged or side-tracked in your pursuit of an acting career? When do you get discouraged, and how do you cope? When "down," how do you overcome it?

_____

_____

17. When you tell people that you wish to be an actor, do they encourage you to do it? What will you say to the skeptics and naysayers?

_____

_____

18. Everyone finds a different way into show business. There are many avenues—a degree in Dramatic Arts, regional theatre, pounding the pavement in a big entertainment hub, and so on. What do you think will be your "way?"

_____

_____

_____

19. What are you willing to do, what are the sacrifices you would make to achieve a career as an actor?

_____

_____

20. As in any business endeavor, you will need to have a financial plan in place. How will you support the establishment of your acting career?

_____

_____

21. Looking at your goals and assessing the reality of achieving them, who is the primary person you will you turn for advice, perspective and mentoring?

_____

_____

22. What is typecasting and how do you feel about it? How can you avoid it?

_____

_____

23. Just like a book that has to sum up and persuade a buyer all in the back jacket copy, so do you have a small window in which to "pitch" or sell yourself. In one sentence, describe yourself as an actor. Example: "I am the wise-cracking side-kick to the romantic lead character."

_____

_____

24. Considering where you are at this time in your life, what is the first step you can take toward launching your acting career?

_____

_____

25. List 5 ways you can gain both experience and exposure right now, in local venues.

_____

_____

_____

_____

_____

26. What monologues from plays, TV shows or films most resonate with you? List 2. (Be sure to keep this handy for last-minute general auditions.)

_____

_____

27. Networking plays a big part in the building and maintenance of a show business career. Make a list of 10 contacts with whom you have already worked. Add their contact information to this list and keep it updated.

_____

_____

_____

_____

_____

_____

_____

_____

_____

_____

28. Visualizing your journey should be as specific as possible so you can outline the appropriate steps to be taken to accomplish what you have in mind. What is the arc you envision for your career? Where do want to start, and where do you want to be in five years?

_____

_____

_____

_____

29. List the 5 most significant goals and benchmarks you feel you must attain to feel successful in your pursuit of an acting career.

_____

_____

_____

_____

_____

30. Beth Grant talked about "learning and accepting" her casting. What type of roles can you realistically compete for? List 3 specific examples of current parts that would be "right" for you.

_____

_____

_____

NOTES

NOTES

Appendix B

Contributors to Sage Advice from Well-Seasoned Actors

MARIANN AALDA

Mariann cut her teeth as a sketch-comedy writer and performer for tough NYC audiences alongside "Forever Plaid" creator, Stuart Ross, as a member of the award-winning Off-Center theater company. She then honed her improvisational skills touring with "The Proposition," which also launched the comedy career of Jane Curtin. Mariann made her legitimate New York stage debut with the legendary Ossie Davis and Ruby Dee in "Take It from the Top," produced by Woody King.

While numerous stage appearances followed, Mariann is primarily known for her work in television. Highlights include a long-running role on the ABC soap opera, "Edge of Night" as the popular (Afternoon TV Award-winning) DiDi Bannister. Mariann co-starred in the films "Class Act;" "Nobody's Perfect;" "The Wiz;" and, had series regular roles on the CBS sitcom "The Royal Family" (as the daughter of Redd Foxx and Della Reese), and three seasons on HBO's "First and 10," along with high-profile recurring roles as the tragically disfigured "Lena Hart" (proclaimed by "Soap Opera Weekly" as Best BAD Storyline of the Year) and Lita Ford, Meshach Taylor's girlfriend on CBS's "Designing Women."

Most memorable of her many guest appearances include being befriended by Brett Butler on "Grace Under Fire," and going-toe-to-toe with Mo'Nique on "The Parkers." Mariann was co-host of

"Designs for Living" on USA, and as a reporter for WNBC-TV/ NY's "Now!" entertainment news show.

In addition to being a co-creator/writer/producer/performer of the sexistential musical comedy, "MOIST" with Iona Morris, other writer-producer projects include "Herotique-Aahh;" and the cabaret act and comedy CD built around her "Black Don't Crack but Don't Try and Spread it Too Thin" essays, playing Ginger Peechee-Keane in the comedy solo show "Occupy Your Vagina!;" and, her comedy web series "Talk To Me, Ginger!"

You can find Mariann Aalda at mariannaalda.com

ROBERTA BASSIN

Roberta E. Bassin is a professional actress, having received high acclaim for her compelling portrayals of an array of interesting characters in film, TV and stage including "Barfly," and Emmy and Golden Globe best MOW winner "Indictment: The McMartin Trial." A few of her many performances in television include "E.R.;" "Crossing Jordan;" "American Dreams;" and, "The Pretender."

Ms. Bassin has also appeared in numreous television commercials and her one woman show, "Amelia Earhart: In Her Own Words" directed by Lyla Graham. Roberta is a graduate of UCLA and holds a California Lifetime Teaching Credential. She is an artist of water color and oils. A dancer since the age of five, ballet and jazz dance continue to be a part of her physical life as does music, having studied and performed on the violin, as a singer, and taken up the piano as an adult. A wife, having married her prom date at nineteen, Roberta is the proud mother of a son and daughter, both graduates of UCLA.

You can find Roberta Bassin at IMDB.com.

JAN BINA

Jan Bina graduated cum laude with a B.A. in Theatre from Mundelein College in Chicago. She also has an M.A. from Indiana University in Radio and Television. She is an actor, casting associate and writer/producer. While living in Chicago, she performed for many years at The Second City; had an award-winning comedy act with Pam Pauly; was a DJ at Radio Station WSDM-FM; and, toured Europe with The Godzilla Rainbow Troupe.

She has appeared in numerous films and TV shows and countless commercials, including the 2008 campaign for the "GABA Language School" that shot in Tokyo. With Lee Murphy, she co-wrote the comedy "Sirens of Seduction" which had a very successful run at *The Victory Theater* in Burbank. Currently she is busy writing and producing material for her website, *In The Trenches Productions.Com*. Jan has been an acting coach for both adults and children for the past 12 years, and, a Casting Associate at Broad Cast for the past 16 years.

You can find Jan Bina at IMDB.com

MURPHY CROSS

From dancing on Broadway in the original production of "A Chorus Line" to guesting as Louie's blind date on "Taxi," Murphy Cross has had a unique, career. Murphy has extensive television acting credits including "Numbers;" "Cheers;" "Night Court;" and, "Family Law." One of her favorite gigs was playing Australia with Peter Allen in his show "Up in One." Murphy is a Broadway acting/singing/dancing alumna of "Pal Joey;" "Bubbling Brown Sugar;" and, "Division Street." Her short film "Blinders" garnered several Festival awards. Now she is co-directing a film which her Upright Citizens Brigade based-daughter wrote called, "Maybe Another Time."

You can find Murphy Cross at IMDB.com

ROBIN DEARDEN

Robin Dearden is a professional actress whose career spans stage, television, film and commercials. Robin has starred in such feature films as "Myron's Movie" and "The Wooley Boys" with Peter Fonda and Kris Kristoffersen. "The Asphalt Cowboy;" "Fugitive Family;" "Joe Dancer;" "Murder One, Dancer 0;" "Earthlings;" and, "Thirst" are a few among her many television movie credits. Her guest-star roles include "Murder She Wrote;" "Generations;" "Nine to Five;" "T.J. Hooker;" "The New

Love American Style;" "Knight Rider;" "Magnum P.I.;" and, "Airwolf"—where she met her husband, 3-time Emmy Winner Bryan Cranston, who starred in "Breaking Bad." Robin also starred in the feature film "Last Chance" (written for her by her husband), which garnered many film Festival awards.

You can find Robin Dearden at IMDB.com

BARBARA DIRICKSON

Barbara Dirickson's acting career includes television, film, commercials, voice-over and a very expansive stage career at the most prestigious theaters. Barbara was a leading lady at the world renowned American Conservatory Theatre (ACT) in San Francisco for 15 years, where she played such roles as Gwendolyn in "Travesties;" Shelly in "Buried Child;" and, Gwen in "Fifth of July." A few of the roles she performed for the Seattle Repertory include Annie/Grace in "London Suite" by Neil Simon; Claire in "A Delicate Balance;" Sylvia in "Sylvia;" and, Kate in "Dancing at Lughnasa." She also graced the stage at the Intiman Theatre playing Julie Cavendish in "The Royal Family;" Sally in "The Mandrake Root" with Lynn Redgrave; Diana Vreeland in "Full Gallop;" and, others. Barbara guest-starred on such TV shows as "The Fugitive;" "Northern Exposure;" "Lou Grant;" and, TV movies such as "The Joyful Partaking in the Sorrows of Life;" "The Victim;" "The Big Picture;" "Lady With a Badge;" and, "Health Sleuths."

You can find Barbara Dirickson at IMDB.com

JUDITH DRAKE

Born and raised in Tulsa, OK, Judith Drake was on a bus to New Hampshire and summer stock the day after graduating from college and has never looked back. Forty-five years of regional, summer and dinner theatre, national and international tours, Broadway Off and Off-Off Broadway, commercials, TV and films, she is still keepin' on keepin' on.

You can find Judith Drake at IMDB.com

MAGGIE EGAN-CUMMINGS

Maggie Egan-Cummings has been a working professional actress for over 30 years. She has appeared as an on-camera principal performer in over 600 TV commercials and for seven years was the on-camera spokesperson for The Disney Channel amassing a credit of 400 commercials for Disney alone. Maggie has recorded hundreds of radio commercials, plus more than 30 corporate training films as the spokesperson or as a principal performer.

Maggie got her first big break when she was chosen from tens of thousands of actors to appear on the first season of "Star Search." It was this show that allowed Maggie entrée to Hollywood. Over the years, Maggie has appeared in over 50 TV shows, including a recurring role in the Sci-Fi hit "Babylon 5" for six years and then continuing her role on the spin-off, "Crusade." Among the many TV shows Maggie has performed in include guest-star roles on Fox TV's "Standoff;" "The Mentalist;" "CSI;" "ER;" and, "Malcom In The Middle," and feature films such as "What A Woman Wants" with Mel Gibson; "Executive Decision" with Kurt Russell; and, "Communion" with Christopher Walken.

Maggie has taught in many professional acting academies and held her own acting workshops over the years in both Texas and California. She is a proud founding member of the *Malibu Stage Repertory Company* in Malibu, California.

You can find Maggie Egan at maggieegan.com

TERESA GANZEL

Teresa Ganzel would best be remembered for her work in the 80's and early 90's. She appeared over 30 times with Johnny Carson on "The Tonight Show" doing sketches as well as being on the guest panel. She played Jackie Gleason's wife in "The Toy;" Bill Paxton's wife in the mini-series "Fresno;" Jeff Goldblum's love interest in "Transylvania 6-500;" and Jim Carrey's boss in the 13 episode-series "The Duck Factory." Other series regular roles were on "Teacher's Only" with Lynn Redgrave and Jean Smart; "Roxie" with Andrea Martin; and, "The Dave Thomas Show." She has had a number of guest-spots including "Three's Company" to over 40 others, mostly situation comedies.

She also has done many voice-overs in radio and animation including "Wall-E;" "UP;" "Monsters Inc.;" "Toy Story;" and, more recently, she has been touring in the play "Viagara Falls: You've Got Hate Mail" on Off-Broadway and beyond. And she recently played showgirl Shar Donay in the film "Expecting Mary."

You can find Teresa Ganzel at IMDB.com

BETH GRANT

Known as a Hollywood lucky charm, Beth Grant has co-starred in three Academy Award winning Best Pictures: "The Artist;" "No Country for Old Men;" and, "Rain Man." She has twice received the Screen Actors Guild Ensemble Award for "Little Miss Sunshine" and, "No Country for Old Men." She also voiced the Academy Award-winning Best Animated Feature, "Rango." In addition to her Academy Award-winning films, her more than 80 feature films include many hits: "Donnie Darko;" "Factory Girl;" "Rock Star;" "The Rookie;" "Speed;" "Too Wong Foo;" "A Time to Kill;" "Our Very Own;" "Extract;" "Sordid Lives;" "City Slickers;" and, "Child's Play." In 2012 Grant starred as Willadean in "Blues For Willadean" co-starring with Academy Award-winner Octavia Spencer and Spirit Award-winner Dale Dickey. In competition at Cannes in May 2013, Grant played the iconic character Addie Bundren in James Franco's "As I Lay Dying," adapted from the classic William Faulkner novel.

Grant is currently a series regular on the new hit "The Mindy Project" for NBC Universal Studios on the Fox Network. Grant's favorite television roles include appearances on "Justified;" "Modern Family;" "Mockingbird Lane;" "Pushing Daisies;" "The Office;" "Dexter;" "Grey's Anatomy;" "Jericho;" "Six Feet Under;" "My Name Is Earl;" "Malcolm In The Middle;" "King of The Hill;" "Wonderfalls;" "Friends;" "The X Files;" "Criminal Minds;" "Delta;" "CSI;" "Coach;" "Yes, Dear;" and, "The Golden Girls."

Grant received following awards for "The Trials and Tribulations of A Trailer Trash Housewife": the Los Angeles Drama Critics Circle Award; L.A. Stage Alliance Ovation; LA Weekly Award; and, Backstage West Garland Award. In 2011, Grant starred Off Broadway in "Tricks The Devil Taught Me" at The Minetta Lane Theater in Greenwich Village. She is the only actress in history to have won three L.A. Stage Alliance Ovation Awards. Other theatre credits include world premieres by Maya Angelou; Romulus Linney; Horton Foote; and, Mark V. Olsen. Grant enjoyed two stints at The Ahmanson Theatre in "Picnic" and "Summer and Smoke"—directed by renowned Broadway director, Marshall Mason.

Grant recently directed a multi-award winning short, "The Perfect Fit," starring Octavia Spencer, Lauren A. Miller ("For a Good Time Call"); Ahna O'Reilly ("The Help"); and, her daughter, Mary Chieffo.

You can find Beth Grant at IMDB.com

JEANNE HARTMAN

Jeanne Hartman's many years of performance on stage in plays and musicals across the country, her acting experience in front of the camera and her studies at the renowned Juilliard School and the prestigious *Centre Lyrique Internationale* in Switzerland prepared her to become a respected acting coach and teacher in demand by actors, agents, managers and producers. A Hollywood acting coach to professional actors for over 20 years, Jeanne teaches the craft of acting in Hollywood and Hong Kong.

Conducting private and group sessions, Ms. Hartman prepares professional actors for film and television roles as well as theater roles. She is also the author of the popular workbook, "The Right Questions for Actors." Veteran actors call it their "new Bible" when it comes to preparing for auditions and productions.

Ms. Hartman uses The Group Theater Stanislavski philosophy. This group became the "Legends in American Theater" including Stella Adler; Lee Strasberg; Elia Kazan; Barbara Loden; Clifford Odets; Sanford Meisner, and Robert Lewis. Her clients have appeared in major film and television productions including:

"Mad Men;" "The Man with the Iron Fists;" "Curb Your Enthusiasm;" "Seinfeld;" "Frasier;" "Friends;" "King of Queens;" "CSI;" "Seventh Heaven;" "West Wing;" "ER;" "Jurassic Park III;" "The Fast and the Furious;" "Tokyo Drift;" "Better Luck Tomorrow;" "Ally McBeal;" "Nash Bridges;" "Judging Amy;" "Walker Texas Ranger;" "General Hospital;" "The Bold and the Beautiful;" "The Guiding Light;" "The Young and the Restless"—plus hundreds of pilots and HBO projects.

You can find Jeanne Hartman at JeanneHartmanActorsDetective.com

ANNE MARIE HOWARD

Anne Marie Howard first appeared onstage in the musical, "Carousel" at age 4. She began producing plays in her backyard shortly after that, and at 14, when the family moved to Davenport, Iowa, she starred in every high school play, musical and variety show. At 18, she moved to New York City to study acting at the American Academy of Dramatic Arts, the Neighborhood Playhouse and the Stella Adler Conservatory. Anne Marie appeared in the Off-Broadway productions "Summertree" and "Baseball Wives." She played Nicole Love on "Another World," and Kimberly Brady on "Days of Our Lives" for many years.

She works regularly in feature films and television series. Recent TV credits include "Castle;" "Criminal Minds;" "Private Practice;" and, "Desperate Housewives." Anne Marie was recurring on the ABC Family series "Make It or Break It." Her feature films include "You Don't Mess with the Zohan;" "The Weather Man;" "Shopgirl" and, "Prince of Darkness." She's been seen in hundreds of television commercials and was the spokesperson for the National Association of Realtors, Ditech and Maalox. She can also be heard in numerous voice-overs on the radio, web, and television.

You can find Anne Marie Howard at annemariehoward.com

SHERRY HURSEY

Sherry Hursey is an award winning actress, vocalist, voice-over artist, writer and producer whose face and voice are very familiar to television and film audiences worldwide. Sherry may be most recognized for her role as Al's fiancée, Ilene, on the long running ABC series "Home Improvement", or Kirsten Dunst's mom in the Universal box office hit, "Bring It On." Diehard fans still think of her as Paula Carson on "Days of Our Lives" or Murray's daughter on the "Mary Tyler Moore Show." Sherry has been featured in over a hundred radio and television commercials and guest-starred in over forty popular television shows, ranging from "The Waltons" to "Dr. Quinn Medicine Woman" to "Touched by an Angel" to "NYPD Blue" to "CSI" to "Judging Amy" and "Nip/ Tuck."

Ms. Hursey has starred in numerous television pilots, four television series and over a dozen movies for television. Her favorites include working with James Garner in the "Rockford Files-I Love LA;" the Emmy award-winning "Friendly Fire" with Carol Burnett; "Hit and Run;" "Lyin' Eyes; "Prince of Bel Air;" and, working with the beloved Walter Matthau in "Mrs. Lambert Remembers Love." Sherry has also enjoyed working as a voice-over artist, allowing her to utilize her diverse voice talents in such movies as: "Shrek;" "Madagascar;" "Polar Express;" "Monsters vs Aliens;" "Astro Boy;" "Country Bears;" "Howl's Moving Castle;" and, "Pom Poko."

Sherry's stage credits have honored her with New York's Outer Critics Circle Award and Drama Logue awards. Ms. Hursey created an award-winning one-hour family musical special that she also stars in "Lilly's Light." Inspired by *Lilly's Light*, Sherry and her partner, Craig Hamilton, founded "Lilly's Fostering Hearts"—a non-profit organization advocating for displaced and foster youth.

Most recently Ms. Hursey became partners in Smile TV, a network dedicated to exclusively positive news and programming and video for the "soul" purpose of smiling!

You can find Sherry Hursey at IMDB.com

DORIS HESS

Doris Hess was in a number of movies, like "Overboard;" "Teen Wolf;" "Naked Gun;" and, TV sitcoms such as "Laverne & Shirley;" "Designing Women;" and, "Days of Our Lives." Her early work was in Improv Comedy at the Brave New Workshop and "Funny You Should Ask." Improv was great training for the background voices she did for most of her acting career. Doris has done hundreds of movies and TV shows.

You can find Doris Hess at IMDB.com

JANICE KENT

Janice Kent has been a professional actress for over 30 years, both in New York and in Los Angeles. She has appeared in countless television and film roles as well as many stage productions and over 150 television commercials. She is most recognized for her work in over 100 episodes of "The New Leave It To Beaver;" as Maryellen Cleaver—Wally Cleaver's (Tony Dow) wife. She also directed several episodes of that series. She continues to act on such shows as "Without a Trace" and Robert Townsend's acclaimed webseries, "Diary of a Single Mom."

You can find Janice Kent at janicekent.com

PAT LENTZ

Pat Lentz is an actress whose remarkable gift for interpretation and communication has made its mark on some of the most prestigious projects in Hollywood. On screen, Pat's includes numerous film and television roles, including appearances in Rob Reiner's "Flipped;" "Desperate Housewives;" and, "Bones." Off camera as a voice-over artist, Pat has been heard on hundreds of commercials, films, television shows, video games, and audio books. Her narration resume reflects work on a wide range of popular and critically-acclaimed movies, television shows, and IMAX productions. Known for her keen ability to navigate complex prose and fast-action dialogue, Pat has been a key voice for WGBH's "Descriptive Video Service" for the blind for twelve years and can be heard on countless films and television shows, including James Cameron's "Aliens of the Deep;" Terrence Malick's "The Tree of Life;" "Return to Mecca" narrated by Helen Mirren—as well as over six seasons of "The Simpsons." She is also the voice of five Joyce Meyer best-selling audio books.

Smooth dulcet tones, spot-on delivery, and spectacular cold reading skills make Pat an industry favorite and a trusted talent for a wide variety of roles.

You can find Pat Lentz on IMDB.com

DEBORAH MAY

Deborah May is a television, stage and film actress. She has appeared in such TV Shows as "ER;" "The Golden Girls;" "Days of Our Lives;" "The Larry Sanders Show;" "Murder One;" "St. Elsewhere;" "The Guiding Light;" "Star Trek: Voyager;" "Star Trek: Deep Space Nine;" "Last Man Standing;" "Dirty Sexy Money;" "Cold Case;" "Malcom In The Middle;" "Boomtown;" and, "The West Wing." Films include Disney's "The Kid;" "Nurse Betty;" "Caged Fear;" "Johnny Be Good;" "The Woman in Red;" "FBI Murders;" and, "In The Line of Duty." Deborah is also an Associate Artist of the Old Globe, where she has appeared in ten productions. She also spent eight years at ACT in San Francisco, appearing in over 25 productions, and nine summers at PCPA in Santa Maria, appearing in over 20 productions. She has also worked on and Off-Broadway and at The Mark Taper Forum, Seattle Rep, Louisville Actors Theatre, the Guthrie Theatre, and the Huntington Theatre.

You can find Deborah May on IMDB.com

IONA MORRIS

Iona Morris has been a working actress and voice-over talent for over 25 years, a director for twelve and a writer since the beginning. Iona has won two Hollywood NAACP Theater Awards, two DramaLogue Awards and one Drama Critics Circle Award. Iona has recurred on such shows as "Moesha;" "The District;" "As The World Turns;" "Passions;" and, "General Hospital." She has guest-starred on "Soul Man;" "Love That Girl;" "Law and Order;" "Cold Case;" "Lincoln Heights;" "The Shield;" "Star

Trek: Voyager;" "Martin;" "The Wayans Bros.;" "Homeboys In Outer Space;" "Cedric The Entertainer;" "Murder She Wrote;" "Hill Street Blues;" the MOW "The Princess and the Marine;" and, many others. Iona was a series regular on "The Adventures of ARK." Her favorite film role was as dancer Nila Fontaine in Tim Reid's "Once Upon A Time When We Were Colored." Other films include, "Ride or Die" with Vivica Fox; "Patient 14;" and, "It's In The Bag"—a short film that has won many international festival awards.

Iona was the promo announcer for the CBS Daytime Soaps, TV ONE series special events Promo announcer for ABC Soaps, and has voiced commercials for "Ford;" McDonalds;" "Susan G. Komen Race for the Cure;" "K-Mart;" and, many more. Iona is the original voice of Storm from the hit "X-Men" cartoon series; Medusa in "The Fantastic Four;" and, Robbie Robinson's wife in "Spiderman," among others.

Iona's theatre credits include, "M.O.I.S.T"—a musical comedy written by, starring and produced by Iona and Mariann Alda through their production company *Al & Mo Productions*; "As Bees In Honey Drown" at the Pasadena Playhouse; "Cuttin' Up" at the Pasadena Playhouse and Cleveland Playhouse; "Home" and "Piano Lesson"—staged at the Denver Center Theatre Company; and, "Blues For An Alabama Sky" at The Sacramento Theatre Company. Some of her L.A. theatre work includes "Holding On—Letting Go;" "Mens;" "Girl Bar;" "Indigo Blues;" and, "Tartuffe." In New York, she debuted the plays "Native Speech;" "Telltale Hearts;" and, "A Perfect Diamond" Off-Off Broadway.

You can find Iona Morris at ionamorris.com

MARIANNE MUELLERLEILE

Marianne Muellerleile is a distinguished actress well-regarded for her vast range of comedic and dramatic work in film, television, and stage.

Perhaps best known for her role as Gloria on "Life With Bonnie" and the axe-wielding Norma on "Passions," Muellerleile's credits number well over 450 and continue to increase as she remains one of the most sought-after character actresses in

Hollywood. In addition to her series regular roles on "Life with Bonnie," and, "Passions," Muellerleile recurred as Sister Dominick on Disney's "The Suite Life of Zack and Cody" and as Nana on the Disney XD hit "Zeke & Luther." Additionally, Muellerleile has guest-starred in over 150 television series including appearances on "Desperate Housewives;" "NCIS;" "Curb Your Enthusiasm;" "CSI;" "Boston Legal;" and, "Nip/Tuck."

Her stage appearances include Brian Bedford's company of "The School for Scandal" at the Mark Taper Forum, and, "The Sound of Music" at the Hollywood Bowl.

She has also starred in numerous features and made-for-television films including "Return to Me;" "Liar, Liar;" "The Terminator;" "Smokin 'Aces;" "Thank You For Smoking;" "Memento;" "Passion Fish;" "A Smile Like Yours;" and, Lifetime's "12 Men of Christmas."

Muellerleile also has a stellar career in voice-over work. A few of her voice-over credits include "American Dad," the video game "Fallout;" "New Vegas;" and the voice of Rachel Lynde on the national radio drama, "Anne of Green Gables." She has starred in over 80 national commercials for companies including Pizza Hut; 7-Eleven; Nationwide Insurance; Frito Lay; IBM; Pepsi; Sprint; Hallmark; KFC; and, Discover Card.

You can find Marianne Muellerleile at mariannemuellerleile. com

SUE MULLEN

Sue Mullen has had a successful career for over 35 years in the entertainment industry. After her fairytale beginning of being "discovered" while working as a hostess at the infamous *Ivar's Seafood Restaurant* in Seattle, Sue moved to Los Angeles, and after two years of study with some of the best in the business, she landed her first national TV commercial and never stopped working. Her familiar face comes from being in over 200 TV commercials and guest-starring roles ranging from Potsie's girlfriend on "Happy Days" to a recurring reporter on "General Hospital." Sue raised her family of three girls, who also had successful TV/Commercial careers and continues to work as an actress.

You can find Sue Mullen at IMDB.com

PENNY PEYSER

Penny Peyser began her career at the infamous *Circle in the Square Theatre* in the original production of Lanford Wilson's "The Hot L Baltimore." Her first film was the Oscar-winning "All The Presidents Men." She was cast in the series "Rich Man, Poor Man II;" "The Tony Randall Show;" "Crazy Like A Fox;" and, "Knots Landing." Other favorite film credits include "The In-Laws," as Alan Arkin's daughter, and Gene Wilder's bride in "The Frisco Kid." Her mini-series and television movies include "The Blue and The Gray" with Stacy Keach and Colleen Dewhurst; "Wild Times" opposite Sam Elliot; and, "BJ and The Bear"—along with many guest star roles from "The A-Team" to "LA Law."

Penny and her husband, Doug McIntyre, co-wrote, produced and directed an award-winning documentary titled "Trying to Get Good—the Jazz Odyssey of Jack Sheldon" available on Amazon.com. Penny is working on the new documentary, "Stillpoint"—which depicts life in a Zen meditation center.

The mother of two boys, Buck and Devon, Penny continues to act on stage as well as in film and television and writes sonnets.

You can find Penny at IMDB.com

ROBIN POLK

Robin has done so many on-camera commercials it is hard to list, but a few include Pop Tarts, Payless Shoes, and, Merrill Lynch. She has done many Off-Broadway plays and she considers originating the role of Miss Fuller in the play "Deep Sleepers" as a highlight in her career as an actress. Robin is listed in the *Dramatists Play Service* publication of the play "Deep Sleepers" by Charles Leipart. Robin is now doing stand-up in addition to acting, because "I love it!" She has her own *You Tube* channel with many short films she has produced, directed and starred in.

You can find Robin Polk at IMDB.com

MAGGIE ROSWELL

Maggie Roswell is an American film and television actress and voice artist from Los Angeles, California. She is best known for her voice work on the Fox network's animated television series "The Simpsons," in which she has played recurring characters such as Maude Flanders, Helen Lovejoy, Miss Hoover, and Luann Van Houten—as well as several minor characters. This work has earned her both an Emmy Award nomination and an Annie Award nomination.

Maggie has appeared in films such as "Midnight Madness;" "Lost in America;" "Pretty in Pink;" and, has made guest appearances on television shows such as "Remington Steele;" "Masquerade;" and, "Happy Days." She appeared frequently in the sketch comedy "The Tim Conway Show" and did voice acting for many animated films and television shows as well as appearing on stage in many plays.

Roswell and her husband, Hal Rayle, established the "Roswell 'n' Rayle Company," creating and voicing advertisements for many companies.

You can find Maggie Roswell at maggieroswell.com

CLAUDETTE SUTHERLAND

Claudette Sutherland began her long theatrical and television career in musical comedy originating the role of Smitty in "How to Succeed in Business Without Really Trying." As a writer, she wrote and performed "Dog Man," a personal history produced by Joe Stern at the Matrix Theatre in Los Angeles. Her solo show was invited to the Dublin Theatre Festival in 1996. Daily Variety headlined the show as "Kansas Dog Man Bites Irish Festival"—an original piece about the American Midwest, greyhound racing and her father. "Dog Man" speaks both to the heartland and the heart.

Claudette's creative writing program is based on writing exercises and constructive critiquing designed to keep writers connected with the practice of their work. She has taught over 2,000 classes and coached several projects to publication. Her work is based on her belief that the two careers of acting and writing are built on similar principles of language and structure brought alive by scrupulous attention to detail.

Ms. Sutherland is a contributor to Los Angeles Magazine and a member of PEN West.

You can find Claudette Sutherland at gotoclaudette.com

DEE WALLACE

Originally from Kansas City, Kansas, Dee Wallace has worked as an author, teacher, dancer and actress in film, television and the stage for over 30 years. With over 100 credits to her name, Ms. Wallace is a true tour de force in this industry, working with countless directors, producers and some of Hollywood's biggest names, including Steven Spielberg; Peter Jackson; Wes Craven; Joe Dante; Stephen King; and, Blake Edwards. Dee's career began in New York where she studied with famous acting teacher Uta Hagen before moving to Los Angeles, where she continued to hone her craft with her mentor Charles Conrad.

Her many feature film credits include such classics as "Halloween;" "The Hills Have Eyes;" "The Howling;" "Cujo;" "Secret Admirer;" "The Frighteners;" "10;" and most notably, her starring role in one of America's most celebrated films, "E.T. The Extra-Terrestrial" directed by Academy Award-winning director and film icon Steven Spielberg.

Her countless television credits only add more cachet to an already illustrious acting career, with starring roles in over twenty *Movies of the Week* and four hit television series, including her portrayal as the passive aggressive matriarch in a very dysfunctional family on "Sons and Daughters." Other television credits include "Grey's Anatomy;" "Cold Case;" "Without a Trace;" "Ghost Whisperer;" and, a recurring role on "My Name is Earl."

As a much sought-after celebrity and renowned actress, Dee has appeared on every major news and talk show and has been featured on "E! True Hollywood Stories;" "Oprah;" and, "The O'Reilly Factor." Her speaking engagements include numerous national and international venues including the *Love and Harmony Forum* in Tokyo, Japan; the Dillion Lecture Series, Unity

Temple; the Kansas Film Commission; Spiritworks; Energetic Healing seminars throughout England, and her own healing and teaching seminars throughout the United States. Dee conducts numerous private healing sessions at her office in Woodland Hills, California.

As an author, Dee has written a book devoted to the art of self-healing. She conducts monthly workshops to introduce people to the healing techniques outlined in her book, "Conscious Creation."

You can find Dee Wallace at Iamdeewallace.com

Appendix C

Definition of Terms and Resources for Statistics

◆ **Pilot Season** is the period of time between January and April when the major TV networks shoot one introductory episode, or pilot, of potential new series.

◆ The **Screen Actor's Guild (SAG)** merged with the The American Federation of Television and Radio Artists (AFTRA) in 2012. SAG/AFTRA is an American labor union representing over 160,000 film, television and radio principal and background performers worldwide.

◆ **Callback** is just that. When you have made it past the first round of an audition, you may be asked to come back for another audition. In other words, the Casting Director will tell you or your agent that you are being "called back."

◆ **Residuals** are payment for the televised airing of taped or filmed work for which an actress is a principal performer, after deduction of the original workday payment. The amount and frequency varies by the type of use and job.

◆ **Master** is the proscenium-style camera angle that captures the whole of the scene in one frame, as opposed to close-ups.

◆ **Agent:** An agent is someone who helps you get a job for acting in a commercial, a television show or a movie, negotiating on your payment when you are hired for an acting job. The agent is paid a percentage of the actor's earnings (typically 10%) which is called a commission. You should never pay a fee to acquire an agent.

♦ **Manager,** also known as an artist or talent manager, is an individual or company who guides the professional career of talent in the entertainment industry. The responsibility of the talent manager is to oversee the day-to-day business affairs of artists and advise and counsel them concerning professional, and sometimes personal matters. You also pay a manager a percentage of your earnings (typically 15%), but never a fee. Agents have the authority to make deals for their clients, while managers do not have the ability to negotiate contracts.

♦ **PR Firms** (Public Relations) work with actors to craft a public image, build name recognition and generate buzz regarding a film, or actor.

♦ **Unions** strive to provide competitive wages and safe working conditions for its members. SAG/AFTRA (representing film and television performers) and Actor's Equity aka AEA (representing live theatrical performers) are the two unions representing actors. These two unions do not function as other labor unions do, in the sense that they do not directly provide employment for the members. Through a variety of programs, activities and industry outreach, the unions work to create an environment in which its members will be hired, and they look after the actor's welfare once hired.

♦ **On-camera commercial** denotes an advertisement in which the actor is recognizably seen as opposed to having done the audio portion, or voice-over, behind the camera.

♦ **Casting Director** or **Casting Agent:** A casting agency is one that works as the middleman between producers and agents. Oftentimes clients in need of talent will contact casting agencies in order to find agency-represented talent. Casting Agencies are not modeling or talent agencies; they offer no contracts and do not charge a commission. The Casting Director holds the auditions or interviews for a job. Often an actor will first read for the Casting Director so the Casting Director can pick the best choices of talent in his/her opinion and move them on to read for the producers or directors, or both. The Casting Director will run subsequent auditions for the producer and director, as well.

♦ **BACKSTAGE** is an entertainment-industry brand newspaper and website aimed at people working in film and the performing arts with a special focus on casting, job opportunities and career advice.

♦ **IMDB** or **The Internet Movie Database** is an online information website related to films, television programs and video games. This includes actors, production crew personnel, and celebrities.

Resources for Statistics

♦ **"Fewer than 2%** of all professional actors actually earn a living by acting alone, and the average annual income of a professional actor is under the poverty level. A majority of professional (union) actors work at a second "day job" to pay the rent and earn a living while pursuing their acting career."—Arlene Schulman, "Careers, Acting, Performing / I Wanna Be An Actress," All Experts

♦ **"Something like 92%** of actors are out of work at one time and the same 8% or so are the ones who do work continuously." —Michael Simkins, The Guardian

♦ **"Only 44% of all major roles** are female characters and the minor role percentages are similar." —2007-2008 Center for the Study of Women in TV and Film

♦ **"63% of the roles** available to women go to 20 and 30 year olds." —2007-2008 Center for the Study of Women In TV and Film

Other Books by Bettie Youngs Book Publishers

Hostage of Paradox: *A Qualmish Disclosure*

John Rixey Moore

Few people then or now know about the clandestine war that the CIA ran in Vietnam, using the Green Berets for secret operations throughout Southeast Asia. This was not the Vietnam War of the newsreels, the body counts, rice paddy footage, and men smoking cigarettes on the sandbag bunkers. This was a shadow directive of deep-penetration interdiction, reconnaissance, and assassination missions conducted by a selected few Special Forces units, deployed quietly from forward operations bases to prowl through agendas that, for security reasons, were seldom understood by the men themselves.

Hostage of Paradox is the first-hand account by one of these elite team leaders.

"Deserving of a place in the upper ranks of Vietnam War memoirs." —**Kirkus Review**

"Read this book, you'll be, as John Moore puts it, 'transfixed, like kittens in a box.'" —**David Willson, Book Review, The VVA Veteran**

ISBN: 978-1-936332-37-3 • ePub: 978-1-936332-33-5

Company of Stone

John Rixey Moore

With yet unhealed wounds from recent combat, John Moore undertook an unexpected walking tour in the rugged Scottish highlands. With the approach of a season of freezing rainstorms he took shelter in a remote monastery—a chance encounter that would change his future, his beliefs about blind chance, and the unexpected courses by which the best in human nature can smuggle its way into the life of a stranger. Afterwards, a chance conversation overheard in a village pub steered him to Canada, where he took a job as a rock drill operator in a large industrial gold mine. The dangers he encountered among the lost men in that dangerous other world, secretive men who sought permanent anonymity in the perils of work deep underground—a brutal kind of monasticism itself—challenged both his endurance and his sense of humanity.

With sensitivity and delightful good humor, Moore explores the surprising lessons learned in these strangely rich fraternities of forgotten men—a brotherhood housed in crumbling medieval masonry, and one shared in the unforgiving depths of the gold mine.

ISBN: 978-1-936332-44-1 • ePub: 978-1-936332-45-8

Last Reader Standing
... *The Story of a Man Who Learned to Read at 54*

Archie Willard
with Colleen Wiemerslage

The day Archie lost his thirty-one year job as a laborer at a meat packing company, he was forced to confront the secret he had held so closely for most of his life: at the age of fifty-four, he couldn't read. For all his adult life, he'd been able to skirt around the issue. But now, forced to find a new job to support his family, he could no longer hide from the truth.

Last Reader Standing is the story of Archie's amazing—and often painful—journey of becoming literate at middle age, struggling with the newfound knowledge of his dyslexia. From the little boy who was banished to the back of the classroom because the teachers labeled him "stupid," Archie emerged to becoming a national figure who continues to enlighten professionals into the world of the learning disabled. He joined Barbara Bush on stage for her Literacy Foundation's fundraisers where she proudly introduced him as "the man who took advantage of a second chance and improved his life."

This is a touching and poignant story that gives us an eye-opening view of the lack of literacy in our society, and how important it is for all of us to have opportunity to become all that we can be—to have hope and go after our dreams.

At the age of eighty-two, Archie continues to work with literacy issues in medicine and consumerism.

"Archie . . . you need to continue spreading the word." —**Barbara Bush, founder of the Literacy Foundation, and First Lady and wife of George H. W. Bush, the 41st President of the United States**

ISBN: 978-1-936332-48-9 • ePub: 978-1-936332-50-2

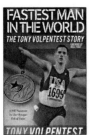

Fastest Man in the World
The Tony Volpentest Story

Tony Volpentest
Foreword by Ross Perot

Tony Volpentest, a four-time Paralympic gold medalist and five-time world champion sprinter, is a 2012 nominee for the Olympic Hall of Fame. This inspirational story details his being born without feet, to holding records as the fastest sprinter in the world.

"This inspiring story is about the thrill of victory to be sure—winning gold—but it is also a reminder about human potential: the willingness to push ourselves beyond the ledge of our own imagination. A powerfully inspirational story." —**Charlie Huebner, United States Olympic Committee**

ISBN: 978-1-940784-07-6 • ePub: 978-1-940784-08-3

The Maybelline Story
And the Spirited Family Dynasty Behind It

Sharrie Williams

A fascinating and inspiring story, a tale both epic and intimate, alive with the clash, the hustle, the music, and dance of American enterprise.

"A richly told story of a forty-year, white-hot love triangle that fans the flames of a major worldwide conglomerate." —**Neil Shulman, Associate Producer,** *Doc Hollywood*

"Salacious! Engrossing! There are certain stories so dramatic, so sordid, that they seem positively destined for film; this is one of them." —*New York Post*

ISBN: 978-0-9843081-1-8 • ePub: 978-1-936332-17-5

On Toby's Terms

Charmaine Hammond

On Toby's Terms is an endearing story of a beguiling creature who teaches his owners that, despite their trying to teach him how to be the dog they want, he is the one to lay out the terms of being the dog he needs to be. This insight would change their lives forever.

"This is a captivating, heartwarming story and we are very excited about bringing it to film." —**Steve Hudis, Producer**

ISBN: 978-0-9843081-4-9 • ePub: 978-1-936332-15-1

Blackbird Singing in the Dead of Night
What to Do When God Won't Answer

Updated Edition with Study Guide

Gregory L. Hunt

Pastor Greg Hunt had devoted nearly thirty years to congregational ministry, helping people experience God and find their way in life. Then came his own crisis of faith and calling. While turning to God for guidance, he finds nothing. Neither his education nor his religious involvements could prepare him for the disorienting impact of the experience. Alarmed, he tries an experiment. The result is startling—and changes his life entirely.

"Compelling. If you have ever longed to hear God whispering a love song into your life, read this book." —**Gary Chapman,** *NY Times* **bestselling author,** *The Love Languages of God*

ISBN: 978-0-9882848-9-0 • ePub: 978-1-936332-52-6

The Rebirth of Suzzan Blac

Suzzan Blac

A horrific upbringing and then abduction into the sex slave industry would all but kill Suzzan's spirit to live. But a happy marriage and two children brought love—and forty-two stunning paintings, art so raw that it initially frightened even the artist. "I hid the pieces for 15 years," says Suzzan, "but just as with the secrets in this book, I am slowing sneaking them out, one by one by one." Now a renowned artist, her work is exhibited world-wide. A story of inspiration, truth and victory.

"A solid memoir about a life reconstructed. Chilling, thrilling, and thought provoking."
—Pearry Teo, Producer, *The Gene Generation*

ISBN: 978-1-936332-22-9 • ePub: 978-1-936332-23-6

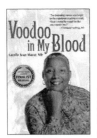

Voodoo in My Blood
A Healer's Journey from Surgeon to Shaman

Carolle Jean-Murat, M.D.

Born and raised in Haiti to a family of healers, US trained physician Carolle Jean-Murat came to be regarded as a world-class surgeon. But her success harbored a secret: in the operating room, she could quickly intuit the root cause of her patient's illness, often times knowing she could help the patient without surgery. Carolle knew that to fellow surgeons, her intuition was best left unmentioned. But when the devastating earthquake hit Haiti and Carolle returned to help, she had to acknowledge the shaman she had become.

"This fascinating memoir sheds light on the importance of asking yourself, 'Have I created for myself the life I've meant to live?'" **—Christiane Northrup, M.D., author of the New York Times bestsellers:** *Women's Bodies, Women's Wisdom*

ISBN: 978-1-936332-05-2 • ePub: 978-1-936332-04-5

Electric Living
The Science behind the Law of Attraction

Kolie Crutcher

An electrical engineer by training, Crutcher applies his in-depth knowledge of electrical engineering principles and practical engineering experience detailing the scientific explanation of why human beings become what they think. A practical, step-by-step guide to help you harness your thoughts and emotions so that the Law of Attraction will benefit you.

ISBN: 978-1-936332-58-8 • ePub: 978-1-936332-59-5

DON CARINA: *WWII Mafia Heroine*

Ron Russell

A father's death in Southern Italy in the 1930s—a place where women who can read are considered unfit for marriage—thrusts seventeen-year-old Carina into servitude as a "black widow," a legal head of the household who cares for her twelve siblings. A scandal forces her into a marriage to Russo, the "Prince of Naples." By cunning force, Carina seizes control of Russo's organization and disguising herself as a man, controls the most powerful of Mafia groups for nearly a decade.

"A woman as the head of the Mafia who shows her family her resourcefulness, strength and survival techniques. Unique, creative and powerful! This exciting book blends history, intrigue and power into one delicious epic adventure that you will not want to put down!" —**Linda Gray, Actress,** *Dallas*

ISBN: 978-0-9843081-9-4 • ePub: 978-1-936332-49-6

Amazing Adventures of a Nobody

Leon Logothetis

From the Hit Television Series Aired in 100 Countries!

Tired of his disconnected life and uninspiring job, Leon Logothetis leaves it all behind—job, money, home, even his cell phone—and hits the road with nothing but the clothes on his back and five dollars in his pocket, relying on the kindness of strangers and the serendipity of the open road for his daily keep. Masterful story-telling!

"A gem of a book; endearing, engaging and inspiring." —**Catharine Hamm, Los Angeles Times Travel Editor**

ISBN: 978-0-9843081-3-2 • ePub: 978-1-936332-51-9

MR. JOE
Tales from a Haunted Life

Joseph Barnett and Jane Congdon

Do you believe in ghosts? Joseph Barnett didn't, until the winter he was fired from his career job and became a school custodian. Assigned the graveyard shift, Joe was confronted with a series of bizarre and terrifying occurrences.

"Thrilling, thoughtful, elegantly told. So much more than a ghost story." —**Cyrus Webb, CEO, Conversation Book Club**

ISBN: 978-1-936332-78-6 • ePub: 978-1-936332-79-3

Out of the Transylvania Night

Aura Imbarus
A Pulitzer-Prize entry

"I'd grown up in the land of Transylvania, homeland to Dracula, Vlad the Impaler, and worse, dictator Nicolae Ceausescu," writes the author. "Under his rule, like vampires, we came to life after sundown, hiding our heirloom jewels and documents deep in the earth." Fleeing to the US to rebuild her life, she discovers a startling truth about straddling two cultures and striking a balance between one's dreams and the sacrifices that allow a sense of "home."

"Aura's courage shows the degree to which we are all willing to live lives centered on freedom, hope, and an authentic sense of self. Truly a love story!" —**Nadia Comaneci, Olympic Champion**

ISBN: 978-0-9843081-2-5 • ePub: 978-1-936332-20-5

Living with Multiple Personalities
The Christine Ducommun Story

Christine Ducommun

Christine Ducommun was a happily married wife and mother of two, when—after moving back into her childhood home—she began to experience panic attacks and bizarre flashbacks. Eventually diagnosed with Dissociative Identity Disorder (DID), Christine's story details an extraordinary twelve-year ordeal unraveling the buried trauma of her forgotten past.

"Reminiscent of the Academy Award-winning *A Beautiful Mind*, this true story will have you on the edge of your seat. Spellbinding!" —**Josh Miller, Producer**

ISBN: 978-0-9843081-5-6 • ePub: 978-1-936332-06-9

The Tortoise Shell Code

V Frank Asaro

Off the coast of Southern California, the Sea Diva, a tuna boat, sinks. Members of the crew are missing and what happened remains a mystery. Anthony Darren, a renowned and wealthy lawyer at the top of his game, knows the boat's owner and soon becomes involved in the case. As the case goes to trial, a missing crew member is believed to be at fault, but new evidence comes to light and the finger of guilt points in a completely unanticipated direction. An action-packed thriller.

ISBN: 978-1-936332-60-1 • ePub: 978-1-936332-61-8

The Search for the Lost Army
The National Geographic and Harvard University Expedition

Gary S. Chafetz

In one of history's greatest ancient disasters, a Persian army of 50,000 soldiers was suffocated by a hurricane-force sandstorm in 525 BC in Egypt's Western Desert. No trace of this conquering army, hauling huge quantities of looted gold and silver, has ever surfaced.

Gary Chafetz, referred to as "one of the ten best journalists of the past twenty-five years," is a former Boston Globe correspondent and was twice nominated for a Pulitzer Prize by the Globe.

ISBN: 978-1-936332-98-4 • ePub: 978-1-936332-99-1

A World Torn Asunder
The Life and Triumph of Constantin C. Giurescu

Marina Giurescu, M.D.

Constantin C. Giurescu was Romania's leading historian and author. His granddaughter's fascinating story of this remarkable man and his family follows their struggles in war-torn Romania from 1900 to the fall of the Soviet Union. An "enlightened" society is dismantled with the 1946 Communist takeover of Romania, and Constantin is confined to the notorious Sighet penitentiary. Drawing on her grandfather's prison diary (which was put in a glass jar, buried in a yard, then smuggled out of the country by Dr. Paul E. Michelson—who does the FOREWORD for this book), private letters and her own research, Dr. Giurescu writes of the legacy from the turn of the century to the fall of Communism.

We see the rise of modern Romania, the misery of World War I, the blossoming of its culture between the wars, and then the sellout of Eastern Europe to Russia after World War II. In this sweeping account, we see not only its effects socially and culturally, but the triumph in its wake: a man and his people who reclaim better lives for themselves, and in the process, teach us a lesson in endurance, patience, and will—not only to survive, but to thrive.

"The inspirational story of a quiet man and his silent defiance in the face of tyranny."
—**Dr. Connie Mariano, author of** *The White House Doctor*

ISBN: 978-1-936332-76-2 • ePub: 978-1-936332-77-9

Diary of a Beverly Hills Matchmaker

Marla Martenson

Quick-witted Marla takes her readers for a hilarious romp through her days as an LA matchmaker where looks are everything and money talks. The Cupid of Beverly Hills has introduced countless couples who lived happily ever-after, but for every success story there are hysterically funny dating disasters with high-maintenance, out of touch clients. Marla writes with charm and self-effacement about the universal struggle to love and be loved.

ISBN 978-0-9843081-0-1 • ePub: 978-1-936332-03-8

The Morphine Dream

Don Brown with *Pulitzer nominated Gary S. Chafetz*

At 36, high-school dropout and a failed semi-professional ballplayer Donald Brown hit bottom when an industrial accident left him immobilized. But Brown had a dream while on a morphine drip after surgery: he imagined himself graduating from Harvard Law School (he was a classmate of Barack Obama) and walking across America. Brown realizes both seemingly unreachable goals, and achieves national recognition as a legal crusader for minority homeowners. An intriguing tale of his long walk—both physical and metaphorical. A story of perseverance and second chances. Sheer inspiration for those wishing to reboot their lives.

"An incredibly inspirational memoir." —**Alan M. Dershowitz, professor, Harvard Law School**

ISBN: 978-1-936332-25-0 • ePub: 978-1-936332-39-7

The Girl Who Gave Her Wish Away

Sharon Babineau
Foreword by Craig Kielburger

The Children's Wish Foundation approached lovely thirteen-year-old Maddison Babineau just after she received her cancer diagnosis. "You can have anything," they told her, "a Disney cruise? The chance to meet your favorite movie star? A five thousand dollar shopping spree?"

Maddie knew exactly what she wanted. She had recently been moved to tears after watching a television program about the plight of orphaned children. Maddie's wish? To ease the suffering of these children half-way across the world. Despite the ravishing cancer, she became an indefatigable fundraiser for "her children." In The Girl Who Gave Wish Away, her mother reveals Maddie's remarkable journey of providing hope and future to the village children who had filled her heart.

A special story, heartwarming and reassuring.

ISBN: 978-1-936332-96-0 • ePub: 978-1-936332-97-7

The Ten Commandments for Travelers

Nancy Chappie

Traveling can be an overwhelming experience fraught with delays, tension, and unexpected complications. But whether you're traveling for business or pleasure, alone or with family or friends, there are things you can do to make your travels more enjoyable—even during the most challenging experiences. Easy to implement tips for hassle-free travel, and guidance for those moments that threaten to turn your voyage into an unpleasant experience. You'll learn how to avoid extra costs and aggravations, save time, and stay safe; how to keep your cool under the worst of circumstances, how to embrace new cultures, and how to fully enjoy each moment you're on the road.

ISBN: 978-1-936332-74-8 • ePub: 978-1-936332-75-5

GPS YOUR BEST LIFE
Charting Your Destination and Getting There in Style

Charmaine Hammond and Debra Kasowski
Foreword by Jack Canfield

A most useful guide to charting and traversing the many options that lay before you.

"A perfect book for servicing your most important vehicle: yourself. No matter where you are in your life, the concepts and direction provided in this book will help you get to a better place. It's a must read." —**Ken Kragen, author of** *Life Is a Contact Sport*, **and organizer of** *We Are the World*, **and** *Hands Across America*, **and other historic humanitarian events**

ISBN: 978-1-936332-26-7 • ePub: 978-1-936332-41-0

Crashers
A Tale of "Cappers" and "Hammers"

Lindy S. Hudis

The illegal business of fraudulent car accidents is a multi-million dollar racket, involving unscrupulous medical providers, personal injury attorneys, and the cooperating passengers involved in the accidents. Innocent people are often swept into it. Newly engaged Nathan and Shari, who are swimming in mounting debt, were easy prey: seduced by an offer from a stranger to move from hard times to good times in no time, Shari finds herself the "victim" in a staged auto accident. Shari gets her payday, but breaking free of this dark underworld will take nothing short of a miracle.

"A riveting story of love, life—and limits. A non-stop thrill ride." —**Dennis "Danger" Madalone, stunt coordinator,** *Castle*

ISBN: 978-1-936332-27-4 • ePub: 978-1-936332-28-1

Thank You for Leaving Me
Finding Divinity and Healing in Divorce

Farhana Dhalla
Foreword by Neale Donald Walsch

The end of any relationship, especially divorce, can leave us bereft, feeling unmoored, empty. Speaking to that part of our hearts that knows you must find your way to a new and different place, this compassionate book of words of wisdom helps grow this glimmering knowledge—and offers hope and healing for turning this painful time into one of renewal and rediscovery. This book is balm for your wounded heart, and can help you turn your fragility to endurable coping, and will you rediscover your inner strengths. Best of all, this book will help you realize the transformative power inherent in this transition.

ISBN: 978-1-936332-85-4 • ePub: 978-1-936332-86-1

Truth Never Dies

William C. Chasey

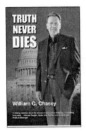

A lobbyist for some 40 years, William C. Chasey represented some of the world's most prestigious business clients and twenty-three foreign governments before the US Congress. His integrity never questioned. All that changed when Chasey was hired to forge communications between Libya and the US Congress. A trip he took with a US Congressman for discussions with then Libyan leader Muammar Qadhafi forever changed Chasey's life. Upon his return, his bank accounts were frozen, clients and friends had been advised not to take his calls.

Things got worse: the CIA, FBI, IRS, and the Federal Judiciary attempted to coerce him into using his unique Libyan access to participate in a CIA-sponsored assassination plot of the two Libyans indicted for the bombing of Pan Am flight 103. Chasey's refusal to cooperate resulted in a six-year FBI investigation and sting operation, financial ruin, criminal charges, and incarceration in federal prison.

ISBN: 978-1-936332-46-5 • ePub: 978-1-936332-47-2

Trafficking the Good Life

Jennifer Myers

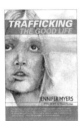

Jennifer Myers had worked hard toward a successful career as a dancer in Chicago. But just as her star was rising, she fell for the kingpin of a drug trafficking operation. Drawn to his life of excitement, she soon acquiesced to driving marijuana across the country, making easy money she stacked in shoeboxes and spent like an heiress. Only time in a federal prison made her face up to and understand her choices. It was there, at rock bottom, that she discovered that her real prison was the one she had unwittingly made inside herself and where she could start rebuilding a life of purpose and ethical pursuit.

"In her gripping memoir Jennifer Myers offers a startling account of how the pursuit of an elusive American Dream can lead us to the depths of the American criminal underbelly. Her book is as much about being human in a hyper-materialistic society as it is about drug culture. When the DEA finally knocks on Myers' door, she and the reader both see the moment for what it truly is—not so much an arrest as a rescue." —**Tony D'Souza, author of Whiteman and Mule**

ISBN: 978-1-936332-67-0 • ePub: 978-1-936332-68-7

Universal Co-opetition
Nature's Fusion of Co-operation and Competition

V Frank Asaro

A key ingredient in personal and business success is competition—and cooperation. Too much of one or the other can erode personal and organizational goals. This book identifies and explains the natural, fundamental law that unifies the apparently opposing forces of cooperation and competition.

ISBN: 978-1-936332-08-3 • ePub: 978-1-936332-09-0

Cinderella and the Carpetbagger

Grace Robbins

Harold Robbins's steamy books were once more widely read than the Bible. His novels sold more than 750 million copies and created the sex-power-glamour genre of popular literature that would go on to influence authors from Jackie Collins and Jacqueline Susann to TV shows like Dallas and Dynasty. What readers don't know is that Robbins—whom the media had dubbed the "prince of sex and scandal"—actually "researched" the free-wheeling escapades depicted in his books himself . . . along with his drop-dead, gorgeous wife, Grace. Now, in this revealing tell-all, for the first time ever, Grace Robbins rips the covers off the real life of the international best-selling author.

The 1960s and '70s were decades like no others—radical, experimental, libertine. Grace Robbins chronicles the rollicking good times, peppering her memoir with anecdotes of her encounters with luminaries from the world of entertainment and the arts—not to mention most of Hollywood. The couple was at the center of a globetrotting jet set, with mansions in Beverly Hills, villas and yachts on the French Riviera and Acapulco. Their life rivaled—and often surpassed—that of the characters in his books. Champagne flowed, cocaine was abundant, and sex in the pre-AIDS era was embraced with abandon. Along the way, the couple agreed to a "modern marriage," that Harold insisted upon. With charm, introspection, and humor, Grace lays open her fascinating, provocative roller-coaster ride of a life—her own true Cinderella tale.

"This sweet little memoir's getting a movie deal." —**New York Post**

"I gulped down every juicy minute of this funny, outrageous memoir. Do not take a pill before you go to bed with this book, because you will not be able to put it down until the sun comes up." —**Rex Reed**

"Grace Robbins has written an explosive tell-all. Sexy fun." —**Jackie Collins**

"You have been warned. This book is VERY HOT!" —**Robin Leach, Lifestyles of the Rich & Famous**

ISBN: 978-0-9882848-2-1 • ePub: 978-0-9882848-4-5

It Started with Dracula
The Count, My Mother, and Me

Jane Congdon

The terrifying legend of Count Dracula silently skulking through the Transylvania night may have terrified generations of filmgoers, but the tall, elegant vampire captivated and electrified a young Jane Congdon, igniting a dream to one day see his mysterious land of ancient castles and misty hollows. Four decades later she finally takes her long-awaited trip—never dreaming that it would unearth decades-buried memories, and trigger a life-changing inner journey. A memoir full of surprises, Jane's story is one of hope, love—and second chances.

"An elegantly written and cleverly told story. An electrifying read." —**Diane Bruno, CISION Media**

ISBN: 978-1-936332-10-6 • ePub: 978-1-936332-11-3

News Girls Don't Cry

Melissa McCarty

Today the host of ORA TV's Newsbreaker, and now calling Larry King her boss, Melissa McCarty worked her way up through the trenches of live television news. But she was also running away from her past, one of growing up in the roughest of neighborhoods, watching so many she knew—including her brother—succumb to drugs, gangs, and violence. It was a past that forced her to be tough and streetwise, traits that in her career as a popular television newscaster, would end up working against her.

Every tragic story she covered was a grim reminder of where she'd been. But the practiced and restrained emotion given to the camera became her protective armor even in her private life where she was unable to let her guard down—a demeanor that damaged both her personal and professional relationships. In News Girls Don't Cry, McCarty confronts the memory-demons of her past, exploring how they hardened her—and how she turned it all around.

An inspiring story of overcoming adversity, welcoming second chances, and becoming happy and authentic.

"A battle between personal success and private anguish, a captivating brave tale of a woman's drive to succed and her tireless struggle to keep her family intact. The reader is pulled into Melissa's story… an honest account of the common battle of addiction." —**Susan Hendricks, CNN Headline News Anchor**

ISBN: 978-1-936332-69-4 • ePub: 978-1-936332-70-0

Bettie Youngs Books

We specialize in MEMOIRS

...books that celebrate

fascinating people

and remarkable jouneys

CPSIA information can be obtained at www.ICGtesting.com
Printed in the USA
BVOW08s1601040214

343720BV00001B/2/P